CW00818780

# THE SURREY HOME GUARD

PAUL CROOK

***Cover picture: Woking Home Guards parade near the Wheatsheaf public house during the fourth birthday celebrations, May 7th 1944. (Andy Stevens) (cover picture)***

**IN MEMORY OF JOHN,**
**WHO DIED AT BÉTHUNE,**
**17TH APRIL 1917, AGED 24.**

*First published November 2000*

*ISBN 1 901706 57 5*



*Design Deborah Esher*

*Published by*
*Middleton Press*
*Easebourne Lane*
*Midhurst, West Sussex*
*GU29 9AZ*
*Tel: 01730 813169*
*Fax: 01730 812601*

*Printed & bound by Biddles Ltd,*
*Guildford and Kings Lynn*

# CONTENTS

# ACKNOWLEDGEMENTS

I would like to thank the following for their help and assistance in the compiling of this book: Michael Trower; Tony Begg (for supplying several of the photographs used in my research and a lot of encouragement along the way); The Surrey History Centre, Woking; The Imperial War Museum; Queens Royal Surrey Regiment Museum, Clandon Park; Chris Rickard, Signal School Historic Library, Fareham; Croydon Library and Local Studies Centre; All England Tennis Club Museum, Wimbledon; Alan and Mary Crook; Peter Crook; Vic Adams; Steve Hellyer; Linda Hatto; Tom Piper; Tony Brine; Bill Pertwee; Jack Wheeler and the Dad's Army Appreciation Society; Brendan Minihane; Simon Sherrington; Hamish Grieve; Roy Cardrick; Peter Sims and Andy Stevens. Most of the material on Woking included herein was gleaned from Andy's research for his own project on the town during the Second World War. To date, Andy's book, entitled "Stand To Woking", has not yet seen the light of day and I am grateful for his permission to use quotes and photographs planned for inclusion in his proposed publication).

Many former Surrey Home Guards and their friends and relatives have written to me with their reminiscences and a special vote of thanks is given to the following:

Mrs R Ames, M Ascher, K Bell, J Booker, G Brine, Mrs J Broomfield, Mrs B Brown, Mr and Mrs J Burrows, B Carruthers, Mrs A Cox, F Cummings, Mrs J Daniells, D Davidson, F Fertig, J Fisher, Mrs J Ford, Mrs I Franks, Mrs S Garnett and Mr H Garnett, Mrs K Grace, D Grew, R Hack, A Haine, D Harman, H Hart, E Hurse, Mrs J Johnson, Mrs I Kerridge, Mrs J King, R Lowther, J Lyons, Mrs M Martin, N Molyneux, D Norris, Miss J Page-Mole, G Passmore, W Peer, Mrs M Pickering, A Smith, Mrs J Smith, D Spong, A Tims, Mrs P Tongue, J Turner, P Webb, Dr W Wheeler, Mrs E Wicks, K Wicks.

I would like to record a special 'thank you' on behalf of myself and Andy Stevens to the late Dennis Batten, ex-Woking Home Guard. Dennis spent a lot of time with Andy during his research and I have been lucky enough to access to the notes of their conversations. Mr Batten kept records of all his activities during his time with the Home Guard and without the help and guidance he provided to Andy it would have been very difficult for his project to have got off the ground and for me to include anything much on Woking in this book.

Information has also been obtained from the web site of the Commonwealth War Graves Commission.

Included within the content of this book are several photographs that have come to me from private hands and whilst I have attempted to contact all copyright holders this has not always proved possible. My apologies to anyone who I have not been able to trace.

*Paul Crook*
*June 2000.*

# SURREY HOME GUARD CHRONOLOGY

| | |
|---|---|
| **1940** | |
| May 14th | Formation of the Local Defence Volunteers (LDV) |
| May 17th | Captain Hill leads first patrol of the Reigate LDV. Spot near the water tower on Colley Hill chosen as the unit's first Observation Post. |
| June 13th | Announcement made that the ringing of Church bells would now indicate that an airborne landing of enemy troops had been made in the vicinity of the Church concerned. |
| July 31st | Name of force changed to Home Guard following a speech by Prime Minister Winston Churchill. |
| August 18th | Kenley bombed. Platoon Commander William Battle, 58th Battalion (Purley) is killed whilst on duty. |
| September 5th | Members of 62nd Surrey (Norbury) Battalion called out to look for parachutists reported as landing on local golf course. False alarm probably caused by beams from searchlights being mistaken for parachutes. |
| September 7th | Codeword "Cromwell" issued, indicating that conditions were suitable for an invasion attempt. |
| November | 81 members of the Ewhurst Women's Voluntary Services knit 71 balaclava helmets, 74 scarves and 66 gloves for the local Home Guards. |
| **1941** | |
| March 20th | B, C and D Companies, 8th Surrey (Reigate) participate in their first Church Parade. |
| May | Commissions introduced to the Home Guard. |
| May 16th | Special Services Section introduced into the 51st Surrey (Malden). To be manned by the younger, fitter men, the Section was intended to become the Battalion's Commando unit. |
| **1942** | |
| February | Compulsory Home Guard service introduced. |
| February 28th | Men of the Lightwater Platoon are shown Ministry of Information films and Will Hay comedies. £5 is raised the cost of erecting a new Headquarters for the Platoon, which the men will build themselves to save on labour costs Spring Home Guards are transferred to RA Anti Aircraft Batteries. |
| June 16th-21st | Home Guard Training Fortnight held in the South East, arranged by Lt Gen B L Montgomery. |
| August | Transport Section formed by 5th Surrey (Guildford) Battalion. |
| September 2nd | Film of the village's Home Guard arriving for duty is shown at a meeting of the Ewhurst Women's Institute. The ladies also see a film of evacuees arriving in the village. |
| December 19th | £28 raised by the Send Home Guard Entertainments Committee sent to the Duke of Gloucester's Red Cross Fund for prisoners of war. |
| **1943** | |
| April | Sanction given for ladies to be enrolled for the first time in the Home Guard. |
| April | Announcement made that the ringing of Church bells no longer indicated an airborne invasion. |
| May 1st | 64th Surrey (Kingston) Battalion formed from personnel transferred from the 53rd Battalion. |
| May 16th | 3rd Anniversary parades. |
| **1944** | |
| September 6th | Announcement made that the Home Guard is to stand down in December 1944. |
| October 22nd | Last parade of the 64th Battalion, Kingston. |
| December 3rd | Final parades held, including one in Hyde Park, London, attended by members of every Home Guard Battalion. |
| December 31st | Home Guard officially stood down. |
| **1945** | |
| December 31st | Home Guard disbanded. |

# CHAPTER ONE -

# IT ALL HAPPENED BEFORE

Although there had never been a "Home Guard" before, the principle of arming the locals to defend their area against an invasion was not a new one.

Many argue that the history of the Home Guard can be traced back to Saxon times but it is perhaps in that late 18th and early 19th centuries that volunteer home defence forces really came to the fore. With Napoleon Bonaparte sweeping all before him in continental Europe, the prospect that his armies might cross the English Channel at the turn of the 19th century led many landed gentry to form armed bands of local men, the Yeomanry, to protect their area and property. The Sea Fencibles were formed on 14th March 1798 to defend the coast of Great Britain. France was again the feared invader in the late 1850s and further attempts were made at this time to arm the local citizenry. Both these scares led to Government recognition for the volunteers leading to an act of Parliament in 1863 regularising the funding of such volunteer bodies and giving the local organisations a place in the structure of Britain's Amy.

With war breaking out in August 1914, many rifle clubs began to form their own units to help ward off any potential invader. Many other such units were raised in towns and villages across the country. The following November, following constant lobbying by Lord Desborough and other notables including Sir Arthur Conan Doyle, the government begrudgingly gave official recognition to a new body to be known as The Central Association of Volunteer Training Corps to coordinate these local units.

The VTC never received any funding from the government. Weapons and equipment were also not forthcoming, the only item of uniform provided being an armband bearing the initials "GR". The initials gave many observers the opportunity to have a joke at the volunteer's expense, describing members of the corps as "George's Wrecks", "Genuine Relics" or "Granpapa's Regiment". The Volunteer Regiments lasted until after the end of the conflict however, some units not disbanding until the end of 1919.

With Hitler coming to power in Germany in 1933 many feared that the peace was about to end and in 1936 appeals were made to older men in Britain to join newly formed National Defence Companies. With no war as such to fight the appeals fell on stony ground and the National Defence Companies never caught the public's imagination and were allowed to virtually fade away.

*Khaki LDV armband. (Paul Crook)*

# CHAPTER TWO -

# THE EARLY DAYS

## ENROLMENTS

On September 1st 1939, Hitler's Army marched into Poland. No one had stopped him when he invaded Austria and then Czechoslovakia and no one was going to stop him now, despite British and French guarantees to Poland that her borders would be secured.

A false alarm made Londoners scramble for the air raid shelters shortly after Prime Minister Neville Chamberlain's announcement of the war against Germany but no enemy planes were to come for many months. Britain had entered a period that was to become known as 'The Phoney War'. It took the German invasion of the low countries and France to stir Britain from its slumbers.

The German advance began on May 10th 1940. On the same day Neville Chamberlain, already ill with the cancer that would eventually kill him, was replaced as Prime Minister by Winston Churchill who, it was hoped, would conduct the war in a much more decisive fashion than his predecessor. The conflict was now coming closer to home and the public at last started to realise the consequences of allowing Germany a free hand. Twenty months earlier many had agreed with Chamberlain's appeasement policies and applauded the famous 'piece of paper' obtained at Munich but now they began to see that more decisive action was necessary if Hitler was to be stopped.

There had been many calls over the previous months for the Government to reinstate the volunteer armies and call on those who were not eligible for military service. The German invasion of the lowlands caused many more to add their voices to these demands. In March Lady Helena Gleichen formed the 'Much Marcle Watchers' to combat foreign invaders near her home on the Welsh border, requesting the local Army Battalion for arms for her 'soldiers'. In other parts of the country demands were being made that Rifle Clubs be formed and trained to ward off any invader. The British Legion put forward its own plans for Rifle Units and even the press joined in the clamour for volunteer armies. Something had to be done, if only to stop the citizenry taking matters into their own hands.

Several high level meetings were held at the War Office between May 9th and 13th and eventually a plan was formulated that would indeed reinstate the volunteers. The plan adopted was suggested by the C-in-C Home Forces General Sir Walter Kirke and it was originally proposed that the General would broadcast the appeal for volunteers. In the event the newly appointed Secretary of State for War, Anthony Eden, made the appeal over the wireless immediately after the BBC News at 9pm on Tuesday May 14th 1940.

"Since the war began" said Mr Eden, "the Government have received countless inquiries from all over the Kingdom from men of all ages, who for one reason or another, are not at present engaged in military service, and who wish to do something for the defence of their country. Well, here is your opportunity. We want large numbers of such men, who are British subjects between the ages of 17 and 65 to come forward now and offer their services in order to make assurance doubly sure. The name of the new force which is to be raised will be the "Local Defence Volunteers" - this name describes the duties in three words.... When on duty you will form part of the Armed Forces..... You will not be paid, but you will receive uniform and will be armed..... In order to volunteer, what you have to do is to give in your name at your local Police Station: and then, as and when we want you, we will let you know."

The initials of the new force gave comedians of the day the chance to poke fun at the LDV, calling them the "Look, Duck and Vanish" brigade or the "Last Ditch Venture". To the press they were the "Parashooters" or, more commonly, the "Parashots". But to those who answered the call the LDV was a very serious business indeed.

Eden's broadcast had an immediate effect. Police Stations all over the country were being besieged by men wishing to sign on as Local Defence Volunteers as soon as Eden had finished speaking. It had been hoped that 500,000 would eventually answer the appeal but within 24 hours some 250,000 had enrolled and by the end of June this figure had risen to 1,456,000.

Eden had not long finished speaking before 70 men had enrolled in Woking whilst nearly 30 had also volunteered in Walton before the end of the day. The Malden area saw 100 offer their services before 24 hours had elapsed. The first volunteer in Leatherhead had arrived at the Police station before the broadcast had finished, asking rather breathlessly if he was too late to enrol. The first man to enrol in Esher was William Curtis, an ex-serviceman. The number of volunteers would rise significantly before the end of the week, indeed Police stations were struggling under the pressure of processing a large number of applications. Joan Johnson remembers her father volunteering. "My mother and I heard the radio announcement of the formation of the LDV. Passing Epsom Police Station a few hours later we were impressed to see a considerable queue of volunteers. On arriving home we found that my father, F T G White MM, had already signed up, being in the first 50 to do so." At Egham the local vicar, the Rev A C Tranter, had dashed through the town to enrol, only to find that two other men had enrolled before him! Although several leading clergy openly opposed fellow priests joining the LDV many others followed the example of Rev Tranter, among them the Rev A Wellesley Orr of St Paul's Church, Kingston Hill and the Rev E R Brittain of Hersham.

Wednesday May 15th saw fifty residents of Byfleet offer their services whilst there were a further 200 more recruits in Leatherhead. Local newspapers, meanwhile, reported that the Police stations at Kingston, Surbiton and East Molesey had been "almost beseiged by ex-servicemen and other applicants". A similar situation occurred at Sutton, where the pre-printed enrolment forms to be completed by those enrolling ran out, requests being made of those queuing for assistance in typing up new forms for later recruits to fill in. Clerks were appointed at Weybridge and Walton to deal with the influx of applications, queues forming outside the two Police stations very early on the Wednesday morning. Members of the British Legion in Cranleigh and Shalford enrolled in the early hours as did the President of the Chiddingfold branch of the Legion, Brigadier-General F Rowley. The Croydon Times also reported large numbers of volunteers, including virtually all the members of the local rifle clubs. This was also the case in Byfleet where the club's rifle range at Silvermere, near Cobham, was put at the disposal of the village's LDV.

Volunteers were asked at the time of enrolling if they had any special skills or abilities that could be useful to the LDV. Any offer of motorised transport was particularly gratefully accepted. Several women also offered their services and were disappointed when they were not allowed to join up. Many units, though, did call on the ladies for help with typing and general administrative work, for example the platoon at Seale under Mr Gilks. Although this type of assistance was invaluable to the LDV many of the ladies yearned to play a more active role. Many of those turned away from the LDV joined rifle clubs to learn how to shoot in the hope that they would eventually be allowed to enrol. Their chance would come some two years later.

All manner of applications were received as patriotism rose to the fore amongst the Surrey public. Eden's appeal was originally intended to be answered only by those with previous experience of firearms, applicants also having to show a reasonable level of physical fitness. These qualifications were not always met! One volunteer in East Molesey was 73 whilst Joan Johnson recalls that "amongst the most enthusiastic were two veterans of Omdurman and the siege of Alexandria. Being in their late 80s they were later retired, much to their disappointment." The 'Surrey Comet' reported that many veterans of the last conflict had offered their services in the Kingston area, saying that amongst them were several who, it was suspected were guilty of "a little inexactitude about their age in order to get under the top limit of 65." The newspaper also told its readers that one man at Kingston had been refused permission to enrol as he was very deaf, despite his protestations that he could see straight. Despite this, many of those who would have failed force's medicals managed to find refuge in the LDV.

It was not only the more elderly who tried to get around the age qualification. A blind eye was also turned towards those of a younger age who dared to come forward. One of these was Gordon Passmore.

"I was living with an Aunt at Hurst Farm, Thorpe Green in the spring of 1940. Her husband, a member of the TA was serving with the 1st/6th Battalion, East Surrey Regiment in France until evacuated from Dunkirk in June 1940. My parents then lived at Steyning in Sussex and my father was also serving in the army abroad.

Although only about 16½ years old and small in stature, I presented myself in my school blazer at an elderly Colonel's house, next to the Red Lion P.H. in Thorpe village (Morley House I think) and was duly enrolled and given an LDV arm-band, a forage cap and an ID card."

The man with the responsibility of organising the Croydon LDV was Mr Norman Gillett, who was interviewed by the 'Croydon Times' for their 1st June edition. "I should like to take the opportunity of thanking everybody who applied to join" said Mr Gillett. "In point of fact the number was almost embarrassingly large. There were nearly 5000 applicants (in the area), and to have communicated with every applicant would have cost over £20. I therefore asked that a notice be read out in churches and chapels and the response was most helpful and I am grateful for it.

The type of volunteer that we have received for the new force is simply amazing and it shows how absolutely solid the country is. One of the applicants actually came on crutches to enrol and another who had been badly knocked about in the last war and as a result is now receiving a disability pension at a high rate was also anxious to be accepted. The Group Commander and I came to the conclusion that these men had done enough in the last war. It is very heartening the number of ex-servicemen who have enrolled and the number of trained men who applied."

Despite already being involved in vital work, many members of existing Civil Defence bodies also attempted to join the LDV. A lot of these applications were turned down but several valuable connections with such organisations were formed at this time. It does appear, however, that there were a few disagreements between members of the ARP and the LDV. In June 1940 the Head Warden for Shottermill and Hindhead, Thorold Harper was moved to write to the Farnham Herald to complain about the attitude of a few members of the new force. "Certain members of the LDV, who ought to know better" wrote Mr Harper, "have related with expanding chest, that they are 'doing a real and useful job', none of the 'ARP stuff' for them! Every trained warden has a good knowledge of gases, their effect on personnel, spray from aircraft, contamination, respirators in all forms, anti-gas clothing, selection and protection of a refuge room, first aid, high explosive and incendiary bombs, message sending, picketing etc etc. Good luck to this new arm of the Service, and I hope that there may be few cases of belittling the work of a body of men and women, who for so long have performed noble work, though not what one might term in the limelight." Some areas saw a much better spirit of co-operation between the two organisations. In some cases this was taken too far for some members of the public, the 'Dorking Advertiser' commenting that several local residents had complained to the paper about ARP members spending too much time with the LDV. The Advertiser replied to this criticism by saying that such ARP workers were only acting as part time instructors or organisers until the LDV had found its feet. In other districts Civil Defence workers were released so as to enable them to make full use of their abilities in the LDV. Major C W Mallett, for example, joined the Reigate LDV were he "proved to be a first rate instructor in musketry and patrols". Mallett was joined in the unit by Mr A J Kitcat who proved particularly valuable through his work on Molotov Cocktail construction and tuition (see weaponry sections). Members of the two bodies would eventually be trained so that they could help each other as and when required.

Among the younger element to offer their services were members of the ATC. In Croydon, Cadets who had previously helped out the town's ARP wardens were now placed at the disposal of the LDV. In Farnham, Captain I Maunsell wrote to the 'Farnham Herald' asking for all boys over the age of 14 to join the local Cadet Corps, with the intention of their being trained so as they could join the LDV or a branch of Civil Defence upon reaching the required age.

Within two days of Eden's appeal 400 men had enrolled in Woking, 200 in Halsemere, 200 in Egham and 300 in the Clandon/Horsley area. By the end of the first week there were over 1000 LDVs in Malden, 400 in Kingston, 850 in Surbiton, 500 in Dorking and 250 in Cobham. In an interview for the 'Surrey Comet' of 18th May 1940, Inspector Reid of the Surrey Constabulary in Esher expressed the opinion that "at least 95% of the men who have put their names down will be of real value to the force". As the Farnham Herald put it, the "Parashots are getting busy (in the Farnham district) and are preparing a warm welcome for any possible visitors from Naziland".

## CHOSEN MEN

Whilst it was intended that the LDV would be administered by the Territorial Associations, those appointed to organise the new force were to be chosen by county dignitaries, such as the Lord Lieutenant and the High Sheriff of Surrey.

The man chosen to form LDV companies in the parts of the county outside of the Aldershot Command area was Captain Edward Tuckwell. Appointed by the Lord Lieutenant, Sir Malcolm Fraser, Captain Tuckwell had served with the Grenadier Guards during the First World War and had been awarded the Military Medal for his part in the fighting around Houlthurst Wood, near Ypres, on April 22nd 1915. At the time of his appointment with the LDV, Tuckwell was Chairman of the Guildford Petty Session Bench and county leader of the Special Constabulary.

Tuckwell's first task was to appoint leaders for Surrey's LDV Companies, all to be based around existing county Police districts. Nine LDV Companies were formed in Tuckwell's part of the county. Amongst the men he chose to lead these local units was Colonel G W Geddes, a veteran of the New Zealand Mounted Infantry and the Royal Munster Fusiliers who had retired in 1934. Lt Col G E W Lane, meanwhile, was given command of the Dorking LDV and Lt Col T D Hassell the Cranleigh units.

A meeting at Wimbledon Police Station on the evening of May 16th was to decide the commanders of some of the LDV units in the greater London area. Major C Micklem was appointed Zone Commander for the area and addressed a meeting called by Sub-Divisional Inspector Bidgood of the Metropolitan Police, telling those present that at least one month's hard work would be needed to organise the LDV. He then went on to ask some of the selected attendees if they would be prepared to take care of the LDV in their areas. Amongst those present at the meeting was Colonel G C Hodgson DSO, who was given command of the Molesey area.

At the same meeting, Col N H H Ralston agreed to look after Malden's LDVs, W P C Tenison (later Lt Col) being given command of the Wimbledon troops. Mr (later Lt Col) M M Hartigan was given command of the Epsom LDV and Mr (later Lt Col) N S Richardson was put in charge of the Norbury volunteers.

Richmond originally came within the command of the Roehampton LDV Company, later the 27th County of London Battalion. On attaining its status as the 63rd Surrey (Richmond) Battalion, Sir Geoffrey Evans was appointed the unit's first Commanding Officer. Evans was a noted botanist and held the position of Battalion C/O until his appointment as Director of the Royal Botanical Gardens at Kew. He was replaced as C/O by Lt Col A E Redfearn on 15th January 1942. Redfearn stayed as Battalion C/O until the Home Guard was stood down.

These gentlemen now concentrated on appointing local leaders to form units in towns and villages across the county. Mr A W Fossdike and Mr A J Mears, for example, were appointed to look after Kingston's LDVs. Brigadier-General S V P Weston, described by former colleagues, according to the 'Surrey Comet' as "an ideal stout-hearted infantry officer" became commander of the Walton volunteers.

Some of the more junior appointments were apparently a little harder to understand. Joan Johnson remembers one such appointment in her home town. "By what means I don't know but the little group of LDVs in Ewell had been put in the charge of a former District Officer in an African colony. Unfortunately his previous experience had not fitted him to the task!" A later appointment was a bit easier to follow, if perhaps not entirely based on military aptitude. "The troops felt that the choice of the Captain in charge was not unconnected with the fact that he and the TA Colonel were fellow members of the Stock Exchange."

Gordon Passmore recalls two of his former superiors. "Our Sergeant was a one-eyed man, wounded in the Great War, who lived on the edge of Thorpe Green, although I do not remember his name. My recollection is that he soon knocked us into shape. The only name that I do recall is that of the officer commanding the unit. Captain Chase. He was tall and thin and I think he had a Colonial Service background. I remember him quite well because he was developing glass cloches at a nursery in Chertsey, which was quite a new concept in horticulture in those days and became extensively used after the war."

Some areas were better blessed than others and, instead of having to appoint men not entirely suited to command, had an abundance of suitable men to choose from. John Lyons remembers one such town. "Camberley had more Colonels per square mile than any where else in the country, so we had no shortage of officers. The local Pearl Insurance collector was our Corporal whilst Jack, whose surname I can't recall but he was in the Royal Irish in India with my dad, became our Sergeant."

## GETTING ORGANISED

With the leaders now in place and several thousand volunteers the next task was to get the LDV into some semblance of order.

This was sometimes easier said than done. Despite the good response to Eden's call in some areas it had been difficult to enrol the required numbers of men, particularly in the more rural parts of the county and appeals were made for new members over the coming weeks through the local press. In some cases, those enrolling in the early days heard nothing further from their appointed commanders, at least for several days. In Croydon, Norman Gillett asked for patience from those who had not yet heard from their local LDV leaders, saying that it had been decided to first concentrate on those areas considered most vulnerable to enemy attack. In Farnham, those who had not been contacted by June 1st were asked to make contact with their local unit, the appropriate addresses being quoted in the local press.

Meetings were now held at local level to organise the LDVs into groups. These groups were generally based on the areas where the volunteers lived, as it was intended that no-one would have to travel too far from their home to go on duty.

Although at that time there were no hard and fast rules affecting the establishment of LDV units, a Company generally had a strength of about 1600. A Company would then usually be divided into four more localised Platoons of about 400 men with a further division being made establishing Sections of roughly 100 men, although this number could be significantly lower in more rural areas. For example, the LDV Company based in Reigate was divided up into four smaller units, ie the Reigate Town Platoon (sub-divided into Reigate North and Reigate South), the Redhill Platoon and the Merstham Platoon. By May 20th 930 men had enrolled in these Platoons, 100 in each of the Reigate sections, 600 in Redhill and a further 130 in Merstham.

The Sutton LDV Company was also split into several smaller units, these having their headquarters at places such as Banstead Golf Club, Sutton Rugby Club, the British Legion Hall at Belmont and Sutton Common Recreation Ground.

Ronald Hack was a member of the Wrecclesham LDV / Home Guard. "Our first muster was some 7-10 days after the call and guard was then mounted at Abbotts Motor Works, NE. of the village proper. Our intrusion in the offices was resented and while we would continue to make our guard at the works, we had to find other quarters." A guardroom was eventually established in the firm's canteen. "At least we had light, water and metered gas, although the use of their coal in the heating stove was a sore point. We also had bed boards and straw filled palliasses, with a blanket each. This was to remain our guardroom until near the end, while the unit's headquarters had to be established elsewhere".

The first conference for local leaders in Guildford was held on Sunday May 19th 1940, those attending being briefed on what was now expected of them. The first meeting of the Limpsfield Platoon was also held on May 19th. Attended by 60 volunteers, the meeting was held in the Girl Guides Hut, "reluctantly but cheerfully surrendered by the Girl Guides who were helpful in keeping the hut clean and acting for a while as messengers" according to the unit's historian. Ken Wicks remembers the early days of his unit in Redhill. "My father, and two brothers enrolled In the LDV as it was known then, on the 6th June 1940, at the Redhill Police station, which used to be in London Road Redhill. They first assembled at the yard of the 'New Inn' Public House, which used to stand at the top of Brighton Road, Redhill. They had the use of a large double garage, which was adjoined to the pub and was at the end of a narrow, but long yard, and the yard was used by the squad their parades and drill in the yard. Alongside the garage were a couple of storerooms which the equipment, such as it was, was kept." Those who had enrolled in Elstead, meanwhile, met on the village green on Thursday May 23rd and listened to Captains Wallace and Thompson outline their duties. In Horsell near Woking, members were asked to attend a meeting in the village hall at 7.45pm on June

7th to finalise the village's enrolments.

## FROM DUSK TO DAWN

Many of those who joined the LDV in the spring of 1940 saw it as a potential chance to get to grips with the enemy. This was not necessarily the way the authorities saw things.

The LDV had four basic duties:

1. Observing and reporting any information of importance to military or Civil Defence authorities in the LDV unit's area, such as enemy attack or infiltration.
2. To delay and obstruct any advancing enemy for as long as possible.
3. The protection of certain vital points, such as factories, railway properties and installations such as telephone exchanges and reservoirs.
4. To act as guides to the regular army as and when required.

It was intended that the LDV should mainly keep a watch, rather than become involved in any offensive action against invading troops or parachutists. The local knowledge of the men would, it was hoped, be of great benefit to the LDV. It was also hoped that any regular troops in the area would be able to make use of this knowledge and that an effective liaison could be established between the army and the LDV when required. In May 1941, Lt Col Richardson, then Commanding Officer of the Norbury Home Guard, reminded his men of their role, expressing the opinion that their local knowledge "makes a member of the Home Guard superior to all strangers in his district, whether they be friend or foe".

It is probable that the first LDV patrol in Britain was undertaken by men in Worthing, Sussex, on the night of May 15th 1940. Surrey men were not too far behind. The first patrol in Redhill went out on the night of May 17th. The patrol was lead by Captain M C Hill, a water tower on Colley Hill being chosen as the unit's first observation post. Unfortunately the tower was found to not give a particularly good all round view and the next night's patrol was mounted in Reigate Park instead. Redhill LDVs eventually manned observation posts at Reigate Hill and Colley Hill (Reigate North Platoon), Nutfield Priory (Redhill Platoon) and Shepherds Hill (Merstham Platoon). Malden men manned two observation posts, those in the north keeping watch from the top of Malden Golf Course, those in the south from Tunstall House. The first observation post manned by the Limpsfield volunteers was chosen because "two fields in the vicinity were considered suitable for air landings". A second post on the tower of a local school was also found to be ideal as it gave a good overall view of the Platoon area. Ernest Powell belonged to a unit based at Guinesses Farm, Woking, having joined up at the age of 16. He remembers observation duties at the top of the hill that is now part of the Hoebridge Golf Course. John Booker a member of the LDV in Chessington, recalls a watch being kept from a hill above Chessington South Station .

Ray Lowther joined the LDV in Chertsey in June 1940 and stayed with the unit until two days before joining the Army on August 6th 1942. "Our HQ was in the Drill Hall in Drill Hall Road, Chertsey. We mounted guard on the Drill Hall, St Peter's Church Tower, the Post Office telephone exchange, the waterworks and on Woburn Hill (between Chertsey and Addlestone, not far from an anti-aircraft battery on which is now Meadowlands Mobile Home Park, on the road to Weybridge). We also participated in a bicycle patrol (rifles slung over our backs) through Chertsey, Thorpe and Lyne. When we climbed the tower of St Peter's Church we always endeavored to start the climb immediately after the hour, half hour or quarter hour had struck, so as not to be deafened when we passed through the clock chamber at the top. We often had a wonderful view of the searchlights and bursting ack-ack shells when the guns opened up."

In Guildford the local LDV were mounting guards on all the borough's water works by June 1st, whilst the Kingston volunteers were in situ on Hampton Court bridge by June 10th.

One of the first tasks undertaken by the LDV was the manning of road blocks. Identification cards were examined and anybody found to be without the correct form of ID was immediately dragged off to the local Police Station. Cases reported to the Police by the 62nd Battalion included the apprehension of an escaped borstal boy. A dim view was taken if anyone tried to get through any

LDV / Home Guard road block without stopping. Several cases reached the civil courts. In September 1940 the Surrey Mirror reported on a case, involving a 'well known Godstone resident' who was fined £17 for 'defying the authorities' after failing to properly identify himself.

The importance of these road blocks in the general defence schemes put in place in each area was not under-estimated by those in command. In Sutton, for example, the Battalion C/O daily carried out an inspection of the road blocks in his command area and exercises were regularly held to test their effectiveness.

Tank traps were also set up in many areas. In Malden, formal training for those manning these posts was started as early as July 1940 under Sergeants Carmell and Oldfield, five posts having been established in the area.

John Lyons remembers his unit being involved in guarding a variety of vital points. "We met as a squad behind the telephone exchange in Park Street, and a couple of nights a week we guarded the sewage farm - with its smell we really were not needed. After a few months, it was decided that Camberley's fire engine needed guarding, so we met in the Drill Hall in the London Road and walked across the road to the Avenue and sat rifle on our knees in the hut that housed the fire engine. Later on it was decided that the Telephone Exchange in Park Street was a more deserving building, a small room at the back convenient for our four hours off".

Although it was to be several weeks before the LDV / Home Guard were to see any sort of real action plans were immediately put in place to deal with emergencies. In Dorking the call went out for volunteers to assist in filling sandbags, an appeal that was answered by, amongst others, the composer Dr. Ralph Vaughan Williams. When asked by Mr Gordon Clark, second in command of the Dorking LDV, why he was helping out and if it was disturbing his work, the composer replied "how can I do my work when my country is in danger?" A similar appeal was made to residents in Cranleigh, particularly those in the building trade, where it was a suggested that a "Volunteer Labour Corps" be raised to help the LDV / Home Guard with sand bag filling and camouflaging.

## TURN OUT THE GUARD

Members of the public had been on the lookout for parachutists for many months and the newly formed LDV had plenty of false alarms to deal with in the Spring of 1940. One such alarm was raised at the end of May by residents in Dorking, although it is not clear if the LDV were called upon to investigate on this occasion. The 'unidentified floating object' turned out to be a loose barrage balloon of which the authorities were already aware. On May 26th the 'Croydon Times' reported that a resident in the Elmers End area had informed the Police that he had seen a parachutist coming down but that on searching the Police found that the report was unfounded.

The existence of a fifth column in Britain gave many serious cause for concern. The Farnham Herald of May 25th reported that "useful plans are being formulated for the defence work, but it would not be wise at the present time to mention them in detail. We have no wish to help any stray "Fifth Columnists" who might be lurking in the neighbourhood." Phrases such as 'Be like Dad, keep Mum', 'The walls have ears' and 'Careless talk costs lives' became commonplace as the general public were encouraged to take care over what they said for fear the wrong person might overhear.

The blackout was strictly enforced and many were brought before the courts to explain why they had not adhered to the regulations. One infringement is here recalled by Guildford LDV / Home Guard, James Fisher. "Whilst on duty in London Road I noticed that every time the air raid siren sounded the curtains in an upstairs window of a tall house moved showing light, contrary to the blackout. This happened on several occasions I reported it to a senior officer. He told me not to worry about it. However, a little while later another member of the Platoon reported the same thing. It was decided that one of the senior men would go and investigate the next time one of the men reported this happening. The system of callout was that one short ring on the alarm bell outside the pavilion would call out the senior officer present, whereas a long ring would call out the entire platoon. On the next siren the curtains were seen to move again and the senior officer was called out. We had no powers of arrest and the officer decided that the occurrence warranted further explanation so the Police were called to the scene. The Police questioned the lady householder who professed to know nothing about it. She then remembered that she had let the upstairs room to a gentleman who was called to explain what had happened. "I must have fallen against the curtain" he said. "But it happens every time the siren goes" the policeman said. "I am not happy with your explanation". The man was arrested and taken away and the LDV heard nothing further of the event."

## UNIFORM

Although Eden had promised in his appeal that all volunteers would be armed and receive a uniform, it would take many months before this promise would be fulfilled.

The first items to be received were LDV armbands, white at first with the initials stencilled on in black ink. After a short while it was decided to change the colour of the armbands to khaki, as it was feared that the white armband would show up too much in the dark.

In Sutton, it was not permitted for a volunteer to be out on duty with a rifle and not be wearing his armband. This was because the lack of uniform could, in the eyes of any invading army, make the volunteer appear to be a 'franc-tireur', or member of an unofficial 'murder-band'. Only a small number of armbands were received at first in Sutton and if a member took one of them home with him other members had to retrieve it as its absence put a rifle out of action as well!

Some of the very early patrols would be undertaken by volunteers in civies, the 'Croydon Times' of June 1st warning its readers that they may well be approached by LDVs doing their turn of duty in their everyday clothes.

Field Service caps came next for the LDVs, these being followed by rather ill fitting denim overalls. In Guildford, both the caps and uniforms were issued on July 6th 1940.

The denims were not very flattering. The historian of the Redhill LDV / Home Guard later made comment on these early uniforms, commenting that "many a short man went to his appointed post with trousers much too long for him, producing a concertina effect, and many a tall man bore a strong resemblance to Will Hay's 'old boy' by wearing trousers like running shorts."

Further problems were experienced by Col J H Mackenzie CMG DSO, Commander of the Ash LDV. "A welcome small number of uniforms has been received" he commented in early June, adding that "the 'have-beens' find that their lower chest has swelled since they last wore uniform and it is somewhat difficult to provide them with the necessary outfit."

These early, rather inadequate, items of uniform were very slow to arrive, too slow for some. John Hunter spent two months with the LDV in Kingston before joining the Royal Navy, who then issued him with his first uniform, his unit of the LDV not having been issued with any by the time he left them for the senior service.

## WEAPONRY

In May 1940 weapons were in very short supply, not only for the LDV but also for the county's regular army. Writing in 'Soldiers of the King', the historian of the 53rd Surrey Home Guard Battalion says that it was generally accepted at the time that there were barely enough weapons available to equip one division of the regular army, let alone counter possibly the mightiest army the world had ever seen. This situation was not helped when the BEF had to leave hundreds of weapons on the beaches of Dunkirk on being evacuated from northern France at the end of the month. Any weapons there were, therefore, had to be issued to the army and the LDV had at first to rely on any armaments they could lay their hands on in their own local area.

Some members brought their own weapons on duty with them. Farmers had a bit of an advantage here as many would have owned shotguns etc that would now be of great use to the LDV. Others might have had hunting weapons, hand guns or perhaps even antique weaponry from past campaigns.

In some cases appeals were made to the general public for the loan of shotguns and / or ammunition. On June 1st the 'Croydon Times' reported that "in accordance with the appeal made to the public to hand in at the Police Station all 12-bore ammunition, over 1,000 rounds have been received at Croydon Police Station." A further appeal was made to the people of Croydon through their local newspaper on June 22nd, this time for the loan of .22 rifles for miniature range practice. "Anyone having in their possession any such rifles and willing to loan them for this purpose" said the writer "please communicate with the Zone Organiser or Mr L H Dowden. Collection will be arranged whenever desired."

The source of some weapons borrowed in Esher might have left a bit to be desired, however. "Weapons had to be hired and ammunition brought and other means used, regular and some irregular, for the acquisition of apparatus and explosives for training", wrote the Battalion's historian.

The weapons taken out on the early patrols were many and varied. One Platoon in Richmond patrolled with leaded sticks loaded provided by employees of the Royal Poppy Factory whilst another's armoury reportedly included antique pistols as well as swords and bayonets.

Pikes were not widely issued at this time, although they were given to some units later in the war. They did not survive in Home Guard usage for very long. James Fisher remembers Guildford volunteers being issued with pikes and broom handles as weapons but says "we didn't mind". One farmer in Wood Street, Guildford, is on record as being issued with a pike thought to have come from Windsor Castle. In Purley, the LDV even received an issue of pikes instead of the crowbars they had ordered. Mr W Rapley also remembers broom handles being issued to the LDV in New Haw, presumably for training purposes.

Amongst the many improvised items put to use by the LDV/Home Guard was the Molotov Cocktail, one of the few weapons available to volunteers at this time (see later section 'Weapons').

The first rifles issued in any real number to the LDV were imported from the USA. These were the First World War vintage P.14s and P17s made in America by the Springfield, Remington and Eddystone companies. The first cases of these were received at the end of May 1940. In the early days, volunteers were also issued with small numbers of Ross Rifles, a Canadian weapon that would stay in the LDV / Home Guard armoury for more than 2 years, despite the fact that it was prone to jamming and was not a particularly popular firearm. These rifles were in very short supply at first and often had to be passed from man to man as new patrols went on duty. However, by May 19th the Guildford LDV were on duty equipped with 150 Ross Rifles with 20 rounds of ammunition, quite a good ratio when compared with some other units. Volunteers in Limpsfield, for example, had, by May 23rd, only been issued with 10 rounds of ammunition per rifle.

Gordon Passmore remembers the Ross Rifles arriving at his unit in Thorpe. "Within days boxes of rifles arrived. These were Canadian Ross .303 rifles packed in solid grease. I was issued with a rifle wrapped in newspaper and had to take it home to clean it up. This I did, with it strapped to the cross bar of my bicycle. The rifle slings arrived some weeks later. We were issued with 5 rounds of ammunition to take home as well."

Whilst there was no official membership ceiling for the LDV many of those recruiting locally were told to limit the numbers they took on according to how many rifles were then available. The Commander of the Malden units, for instance was told on May 21st that 100 rifles had been allocated to his group and that volunteers should be enrolled at a rate of 3 men per rifle. A similar figure was given to the C/O of the Esher LDV. However, by the end of May 172 men had enlisted despite there being only 35 rifles available to the volunteers.

Ammunition was so short in Reigate that only five rounds were issued to those on duty in the early days. Instructions were also given that these rounds were only to be inserted into weapons when the men were confronted by the enemy. Once the five rounds had been expended, the men were told to rattle the bolt of the rifle to give the enemy the impression that the weapon was being reloaded.

It was several days before some units were well enough equipped to perform any sort of patrol or guard duty. May 23rd saw the first issue of rifles to the Cobham LDV, their first patrol being mounted on the same day.

The end of May saw weapons begin to arrive at a greater rate. May 31st, for example saw the arrival at Malden Police Station of 150 rifles with ammunition, all to be distributed to volunteers that same evening.

Some units continued to acquire weaponry that had not been used in anger for many a year. In June 1940, a Platoon in Purley managed to obtain an 1895 vintage .303 Martini rifle, a long Lee-Enfield dated 1909 and an SMLE rifle, the latter complete with bayonet, scabbard, pull-through and oil bottle. The Battalion historian later noted that "this last weapon was long to be the pride of C Platoon."

It was to be several months, though, before the LDV / Home Guard could be considered as fully equipped and able to play an effective role in the defence of their country.

## TRAINING

A large number of ex-servicemen had enrolled in the LDV in its first few weeks. The authorities were now to make use of these experienced men. No official method of training the new citizen's army had yet been established and it was soon decided to let the older members train those with less experience.

Many units took advantage of offers of assistance from officers from previous campaigns. In Norbury, Wing Commander (RFC) Marten-Smith took the first drill sessions of the town's LDV whilst Col W F Hanna offered his services to the LDV in Esher. Hanna had previously been an instructor at the Army's Staff College.

It was not only the officers who trained the new recruits. Training was often undertaken by 'ordinary' LDVs who had some previous knowledge of their subject. This method of training did not always work out. James Fisher's father seems to have run into a spot of bother having been roped in as an instructor in Stoke Park, Guildford. "As my father had previous military experience he was used by the LDV for instruction purposes. One day another instructor was giving rifle instruction to the Platoon in the pavilion. The headquarters had use of a combustion stove. During the training session one of the LDVs was on the floor being told how to fire his rifle and was given the usual instruction 'squeeze and pull by the instructor. Unfortunately a bullet was in the rifle. The shot hit the stove, ricocheted off it and was deflected towards my father, grazing him on the forehead. 'What is the first thing you should do when giving instruction in rifle use?', my father asked the instructor. 'You should always give the order 'port arms for inspection", he continued. This order had not been given and it could be said my father had a lucky escape.

Bill Wilson was in the LDV / Home Guard in Epsom and remembers being on duty for five nights with a rifle and ammunition, despite the fact that by that time nobody had told him what to do with his weapon. Bill also recalls a rifle inspection during which a high ranking officer found a spider in one volunteer's rifle butt.

To combat the evident shortfalls, rifle practice was set up at local ranges, such as the one at Silvermere, and at Bisley, where units from all over the South East were trained. In Malden a Bombing Course was arranged for members on June 15th 1940 as other aspects of LDV / Home Guard work began to be taught by instructors. Courses were also planned in the use of weapons such as the Lewis and Bren Guns.

New recruits continued to roll in throughout the spring and summer of 1940. By the end of July there were over 1600 LDVs in Malden and more than 1200 in Camberley.

## RENAMING

On July 14th 1940 the Prime Minister, Winston Churchill, broadcast to the world. In his speech Churchill praised the regular forces but then went on to add that in support of the Army the country had "more than a million of the Local Defence Volunteers, or, as they are much better called, the 'Home Guard'."

The term 'Home Guard' had never been heard before but this new name for the LDV was thought by many to be more appropriate. The name stuck and on July 31st the LDV officially became the Home Guard.

In August came the announcement that the original LDV units would now all be affiliated to county Regiments. The old units would be renamed accordingly. LDV Companies became Home Guard Battalions, LDV Platoons became Home Guard Companies and Sections became Platoons. Home Guard Platoons could now be sub-divided into Sections, often for particular purposes, such as first aid, stretcher bearing, motorcycle dispatch or signalling.

*Croydon men marching through the town shortly after the LDV was first raised.*
*(Croydon Local Studies Library)*

*SR London West Divisional Superintendent JE Sharpe and LWD Engineer FE Campion fire the first shots on Woking's miniature range. (Southern Railway)*

# CHAPTER THREE -

# ON GUARD

## THE BATTLE OF BRITAIN

The British Expeditionary Force was evacuated from Dunkirk at the end of May 1940 and, with Paris falling on June 14th 1940, many feared that Hitler's next move would be to invade the British Isles. But first he had to gain control of the skies by defeating the RAF.

The Battle of Britain is now recognised to have started on July 10th 1940. At first, the Luftwaffe concentrated its efforts on attacking shipping off the coast of Southern England in an attempt to draw British fighter planes into battle without going too far from their bases in northern France. The raids on British airfields and radar stations would not start in earnest until the beginning of August.

The Home Guard were to play a rather peripheral role in the Battle, although they went into action at every possible opportunity (the railway junction at Redhill seems to have been a major target for the Luftwaffe; the local Home Guard were regularly called out, sometimes as often as six times in 24 hours).

Several alarms were raised in the Home Counties as 'parachutists' were reported landing in Britain. These were mainly false alarms, the only parachutists to descend on the British Isles being those from aircraft shot down by the RAF. On August 20th, members of the 55th (Sutton and Cheam) Battalion were called out to look for 'parachutists' reported landing nearby. Members of the 53rd Battalion were similarly called out on the night of August 26th/27th. Although they also found no trace of any parachutists it was later reported that the men could have come from a shot down aircraft and been picked up in another part of the county. These scares lasted well into the summer. In Norbury, for example, the local Home Guard were turned out on the night of September 5th when paratroops were reported as having landed on a local golf course. It was later decided that the illusion of parachutes had been created by the crossing of searchlight beams.

On August 23rd 1940 the Surrey Mirror reported how the Home Guard were on hand when a Coastal Command crew had to bale out over Surrey. "The Home Guard were so quickly on the scene that they almost seemed to be underneath the airmen as they drifted down!".

Although they were not really supposed to be firing at enemy aircraft, August 18th 1940 saw members of the Addington Home Guard go into action against the Luftwaffe. Dornier Do17s of Kampfgeschwader (Bomber Group) 76 had attacked Kenley airfield in the early afternoon, causing extensive damage to several hangars and destroying many aircraft in the process. Several of the bombers were lost during the raid. One particular aircraft was hit several times, firstly by a Bofors shell from the airfield's anti-aircraft guns and then by Hurricanes of 111 Squadron. The aircraft limped on and then found itself being fired on by members of the Addington Home Guard. The story was reported in 'The War Weekly' under the heading 'Home Guard Shoot Down Nazi Raider'. The bomber fell to ground at Leaves Green. All five crew members were captured, two badly burnt and two more seriously injured. Despite the Home Guard's claims that they fired some 180 rounds at the Dornier it is unlikely that it would have been brought down solely by the unit's Lee Enfields. However, it made good reading that a front line German bomber had been shot down by Britain's part time army.

The attack on Kenley lead to several Battalions in the area being called out for duty. Entries in the diary of the 55th (Sutton and Cheam) Battalion show that all four Companies were manning road blocks in the area that evening until 'Zone stand down' was ordered at 22.20 hours. However, the only fatality due to enemy action within the eastern sector of the 58th Battalion occurred that night with the death of Platoon C/O W Battle, who was killed by an enemy bomb whilst on duty at Kenley.

On August 30th 1940, the Surrey Advertiser carried a report about the 'destruction' of a Heinkel He111, written by a reporter who was also a member of the Home Guard. The Heinkel was on its way to bomb Coventry and crashed in Caterham on Tuesday August 27th. The crew were eventually captured unhurt.

The battle progressed onwards through August and September. 'Eagle Day' (Adler Tag), the day of the great offensive by the Luftwaffe, was postponed at least twice but eventually came about on August 13th. It was not a good day for the Luftwaffe as they lost 45 planes during the day's fighting. August 15th was even worse for the Germans, 75 aircraft being shot down during the day's fighting. The battle was drifting from Germany's grasp. The next four weeks or so would be vital if the planned invasion was to go ahead.

During August, September, October and November 1940, a log book was kept by V Zone, in which was recorded all reports received from the Zone's V1, V2, V3, V4 and V5 Battalions during these vital months.

Reports were made by telephone to Zone Headquarters by each of these Battalions, whether anything was happening or not. For example, the entries for the 11am reports on August 29th 1940 from the 5 Battalions read as follows:-

V1 - Low flying plane during night. No bombs, no casualties
V2 - Air activity. No bombs. No casualties.
V3 - Moderate air activity during night. Accidental discharge of rifle in Fac tory Unit of H.G. caused 3 casualties. Men now in hospital. 1 injured in both legs. 1 injured in both legs. 1 in ankle & 1 in thigh.
V4 - Air activity during night. Nothing to report. No casualties.
V5 - Nothing to report. No casualties.

The beginning of September saw the Battalions having a bit more to report. On September 3rd V2 Battalion reported that two parachutists had been seen over Epsom at 12 o'clock the previous night and that the matter had been referred to the local Police. That same morning, the Commanding Officer of V5 (Wimbledon) wrote to Zone HQ to advise that bombs had fallen in the Battalion area during the night and that he believed that one of them had been aimed at Morden Underground Station. "The flashings from the electric trains at this Station are very conspicuous" he wrote, "and it is suggested by C.O. that the Railway Company should be advised to use some form of screen if that were possible". V4 Battalion had a slightly different problem, having been informed by the local Police that 3 Dutchmen, "believed to be enemy agents", had landed at Dymchurch, Kent and "were making their way inland."

Arrangements had been made earlier in the summer as to how the Home Guard and other UK based troops would be called out if an invasion ever took place. On June 13th 1940 an order had given banning the ringing of church bells. From that day on the bells would be rung only to signify that an airborne attack had taken place in the vicinity of the church concerned. It was stressed that the bells were not to be rung solely because a neighbouring church had rung theirs.

A code-word, 'Cromwell', was established to warn home-based troops if it were at any time felt that conditions were right for an invasion of the British Isles.

A series of further codewords was also established to indicate the state of readiness units should attain at any given moment as follows:-

1. Alert - When an invasion is unlikely in the immediate future but raids are expected.
2. Stand To - When conditions are particularly favourable for invasion.
3. Action Stations - Will be ordered when there is an immediate threat of invasion.
4. Bugbear - Indicates a sea-borne raid, possibly with air raids. Bugbear is a codeword that is not to be used at Battalion or lower level and is not to be used on exercise. When issued an indication of the locality will also be given. When the threat is over Bugbear Stand Down will be ordered.
5. Bouncer - Warning that Bugbear may be issued shortly.
6. Migration - Followed by a number indicates degree of suitability of weather for airborne raids. 1 Suitable, 2 Possible, 3 Unsuitable.

(Nos, 4 – 6 were mainly intended for use by coastal Battalions in the South East Army area)

On the issue of any of these codewords each of the Battalion, Company or Platoon Commanders would ensure that his men were fully prepared to meet the situation indicated.

## CROMWELL

The course of the battle changed on September 7th 1940 as German bombers launched their first raids on London. Additionally, the build up of German invasion barges in the coastal ports of Northern France had long been a source of concern to the Chiefs of Staff and the overall situation had reached such a point that, at 8.07pm that day, the code-word 'Cromwell' was issued and home based troops went on full alert.

The Home Guard were not really meant to be greatly affected by the issue of 'Cromwell'. However, Home Guards from all parts of the country turned out virtually immediately, many answering the call of the church bells that were mistakenly rung in many districts. A large number of Home Guards believed that an invasion had actually taken place and were now preparing to fight off the enemy.

Not everyone knew what was going on that day. Ronald Hack remembers the night's events in Wrecclesham. "Although we heard no church bells, we found ourselves erecting a road block between the two Passmore bridges. All were stopped and checked for Identity Cards. We received much ribald comment, as those we knew perfectly well had also to identify themselves and their mission. They were stopped at gun point and I think they would have been more civil had they realised those pointing rifles were loaded with live ammunition. We kept at it well over our usual parade time and continued until a message of cancellation was received by dispatch rider. So it was home without explanation to a late and overcooked lunch with wives moaning."

Another problem seems to have arisen in Epsom. Mrs Pickering, whose father was in the local Home Guard recalls that "to alert the troops a certain set of flags were issued to be run up the flag pole on the tower of Christ Church. The chart illustrating the message that was to be conveyed was not very clearly written, and as neither of the Home Guards on duty had brought his glasses, no message could be sent from the tower."

The Limpsfield HG had arranged an exercise for September 7/8th which was to be held in conjunction with locally stationed Canadian troops. The Canadians were to play the part of paratroopers and the Limpsfield Home Guard were to 'round them up'. When the exercise had finished, several of the men noticed German planes overhead, some counting as many as 90 to 100 aircraft. The following morning they received a message from the Company Commander saying "the balloon's up" and that all posts were to go on Stand To.

V Zone's log book for September 8th carries the following report. "Soon after 17hrs yesterday, a heavy air bombardment of London Area, particularly the Docks, commenced. Big fires visible in direction of Docks from East Molesey. Information received that troops and H.G.s in Aldershot Command were asked to stand-to. Instructions issued from V. Zone H.G. to all Battalions to be prepared for Stand-to order."

The invasion, of course, never came but home based troops remained on full alert for a further twelve days. On September 15th Germany launched its largest attack yet against London and the South East. The attack was repelled, 60 German planes being shot down by the RAF. Germany's change of tactics had proved expensive. The move away from bombing the airfields had allowed the RAF to regroup and, with the invasion needing to go ahead before the weather changed, Hitler had to admit defeat. The Battle of Britain, which officially ended on October 31st 1940, was won.

Britain no longer faced an immediate threat of invasion but the bombing would continue for many months yet. London, for example, would be hit virtually every night for the next eight months.

## CARRYING ON

The Home Guard would go on to perform many more acts of bravery over the coming months, often during periods of extreme danger. On September 27th 1940, Mr H F H Tidy, a member of the Limpsfield HG, used his body to help protect Mr E R Pease when incendiary bombs fell on Mr Pease's home. Mr Tidy was working there when the air raid took place. He was awarded the C in C's

Certificate for Gallantry.

Two members of the 61st (Norwood) Battalion, Volunteer A E Pritchard and Lance Corporal G Howard, were commended for their work during an air raid on the night of January 11th 1941 when both men rescued members of the public from severely damaged properties.

The conflict was too much for some. James Fisher can remember one particular night in Guildford when he found himself on duty with a younger, somewhat inexperienced recruit. "In the distance we could see the red of incendiary bombs falling on London but all of a sudden I heard something heavier falling. Later in the night the Platoon were called to attend at Merrow Woods. There, hanging in the trees from a parachute, was a 1000lb bomb. My young colleague, obviously frightened by what he had been through, failed to turn out for his next turn of duty the following day and was never seen at any further parades." Members of B Company in Sutton had a similarly frightening experience. Whilst keeping watch from a local hospital they watched a parachute falling to earth. Narrowly missing the hospital roof, it travelled on to hit an out-building with a loud bang. The parachute had been carrying a land mine.

A raid on London and the surrounding areas on the night of April 16/17th 1941 was particularly bad and left 1,179 people dead, including 11 members of the 57th Surrey (Mitcham) Battalion. May 10th 1941 would see London's worst night of the war. After that dreadful night, though, the Luftwaffe's attentions were turned elsewhere as Germany attempted to move eastwards into Russia, a move that was also destined to fail.

The Home Guard, though, remained vigilant. Log books continued to be maintained, including one kept by the Ockley Home Guard, F Company 7th Surrey (Dorking) Battalion Home Guard. Guard Commanders were instructed to write down the names of those men on duty, together with any remarks necessary. They were also asked to the night's report before leaving the guard room. Among the reports made is one of the capture of a German pilot, Karl Bruning at Dene Farm, Ockley on March 12th 1941. Bruning had been flying a Heinkel He111 on its way to bomb Birkenhead. Bruning was the only survivor from the four man crew, although he too was badly injured. He was captured soon after parachuting from his doomed plane and was handed over to the Ockley Home Guard. On duty that night were Sgt C Millett, E Hawtin, W Bolter and R Braveny. The entry in the log book reads "Prisoner of War – Kreigsgefangener – Bruning".

The Home Guard did not slow down for one minute and by January 1942 it was being recorded that picket duties in Guildford had become rather 'heavy', the average member spending one night out of every five in bed! However, LDVs / Home Guards would usually do a turn of duty every one night in four. This would either mean going out on patrol or looking after an installation of particular importance within the Company area.

In Bagshot, John Burrows remembers that one of his Platoon's duties was "guarding the gas canisters in a compound on the Bracknell to Ascot road at Harmans Water. The Home Guards were picked up by regular soldiers and they then took over the guard duties from the regulars between the hours of 10pm and 7am. This guard was performed once the regulars had begun to be more needed in Europe, each man being on duty there approximately one night in seven." They also had to guard the telephone exchange in Bagshot town centre.

In West Horsley, the Fullers Farm Platoon would send out four men on patrol each night. "They had the job of guarding the ammunition stored up on the hills and alongside the road, ready for the expected invasion, if it should come."

In the very early days, LDV members in Reigate were given the task of ensuring the security of the telephone exchanges at Redhill, Reigate and Merstham. Members of the 8th Battalion were later given more extensive duties, including the protection of railway bridges and level crossings in the area.

In the early days, members of the 63rd Battalion were called on to provide nightly guards on the Thames bridges in their territory and on such historic premises as Kew Observatory and Wick House, once the residence of Sir Joshua Reynolds. By January 15th 1942 the Battalion's C Company had been given the tasks of patrolling the Royal Mid-Surrey Golf Course and the Royal Botanical Gardens at Kew. D Company were responsible for the defence of Kew Bridge.

In Guildford, the 4th Battalion was given responsibility for defence of the GHQ Stop Line within the Borough's boundary on July 31st 1941, whilst the Stoke Park Platoon were detailed to guard the town's London Road station.

*Southern Railway men keeping a watch for the enemy at Deepdene.*
*(Southern Railway/Surrey History Centre)*

*The Dornier Do17 brought down on August 18th 1940.*

*Another picture of Southern Railway men keeping a watch at Deepdene. (Southern Railway/Surrey History Centre)*

*Southern Railway men on their way back from duty. (Southern Railway/Surrey History Centre)*

*The Stoke Park Platoon, Guildford (James Fisher is second from the right, back row). (James Fisher)*

*Members of the Compton and Puttenham Home Guard. (Gale and Polden/Tony Begg)*

# CHAPTER FOUR - THE BATTALIONS

Britain's Home Guard was 'divided up' into seven Command areas. These were the Scottish, Northern, Eastern, Western, Southern, South Eastern and London Commands. Each of these areas was then also divided, into smaller areas such as Zones, Sectors, Districts or Sub-Districts.

By the time the Home Guard was stood down in December 1944 there had been 29 different Battalions covering the county of Surrey. These Battalions were based within two different Command areas, London and Southern Eastern.

The Battalions, and the Command areas they were in, were as follows:-

(A) South Eastern Command:

| | | |
|---|---|---|
| 1st | CAMBERLEY | Blackdown Sub-District, Aldershot District |
| 2nd | FARNHAM | Bordon Sub-District, Aldershot District |
| 3rd | WEYBRIDGE | Dorking Sub-District, N. Kent & Surrey District |
| 4th | GUILDFORD | Dorking Sub-District, N. Kent & Surrey District |
| 5th | BRAMLEY | Dorking Sub-District, N. Kent & Surrey District |
| 6th | LEATHERHEAD | Dorking Sub-District, N. Kent & Surrey District |
| 7th | DORKING | Dorking Sub-District, N. Kent & Surrey District |
| 8th | REIGATE | Dorking Sub-District, N. Kent & Surrey District |
| 9th | OXTED | Dorking Sub-District, N. Kent & Surrey District |
| 10th | EGHAM AND CHERTSEY | Dorking Sub-District, N. Kent & Surrey District |
| 11th | WOKING | Blackdown Sub-District, Aldershot District |
| 12th | 3rd SOUTHERN RAILWAY | Aldershot District |
| 13th | ADMIRALTY SIGNALS ESTABLISHMENT | Bordon Sub-District, Aldershot District |

(B) London Command:

| | | |
|---|---|---|
| 32nd | CROYDON | Z Sector (Zone) South East Sub-District |
| 33rd | COUNTY BOROUGH OF CROYDON | Z Sector (Zone) South East Sub-District |
| 51st | MALDEN | V Sector (Zone) South West Sub-District |
| 52nd | SURBITON | V Sector (Zone) South West Sub-District |
| 53rd | WESTON GREEN | V Sector (Zone) South West Sub-District |
| 54th | WIMBLEDON | V Sector (Zone) South West Sub-District |
| 55th | SUTTON AND CHEAM | W Sector (Zone) South West Sub-District |
| 56th | EPSOM AND BANSTEAD | W Sector (Zone) South West Sub-District |
| 57th | MITCHAM | W Sector (Zone) South West Sub-District |
| 58th | PURLEY | Z Sector (Zone) South East Sub-District |
| 59th | ADDINGTON | Z Sector (Zone) South East Sub-District |
| 60th | CROYDON | Z Sector (Zone) South East Sub-District |
| 61st | NORWOOD | Z Sector (Zone) South East Sub-District |
| 62nd | NORBURY | Z Sector (Zone) South East Sub-District |
| 63rd | RICHMOND | V Sector (Zone) South West Sub-District |
| 64th | KINGSTON | V Sector (Zone) South West Sub-District |

It was some time before the organisation of the Home Guard reached the above state. Not all

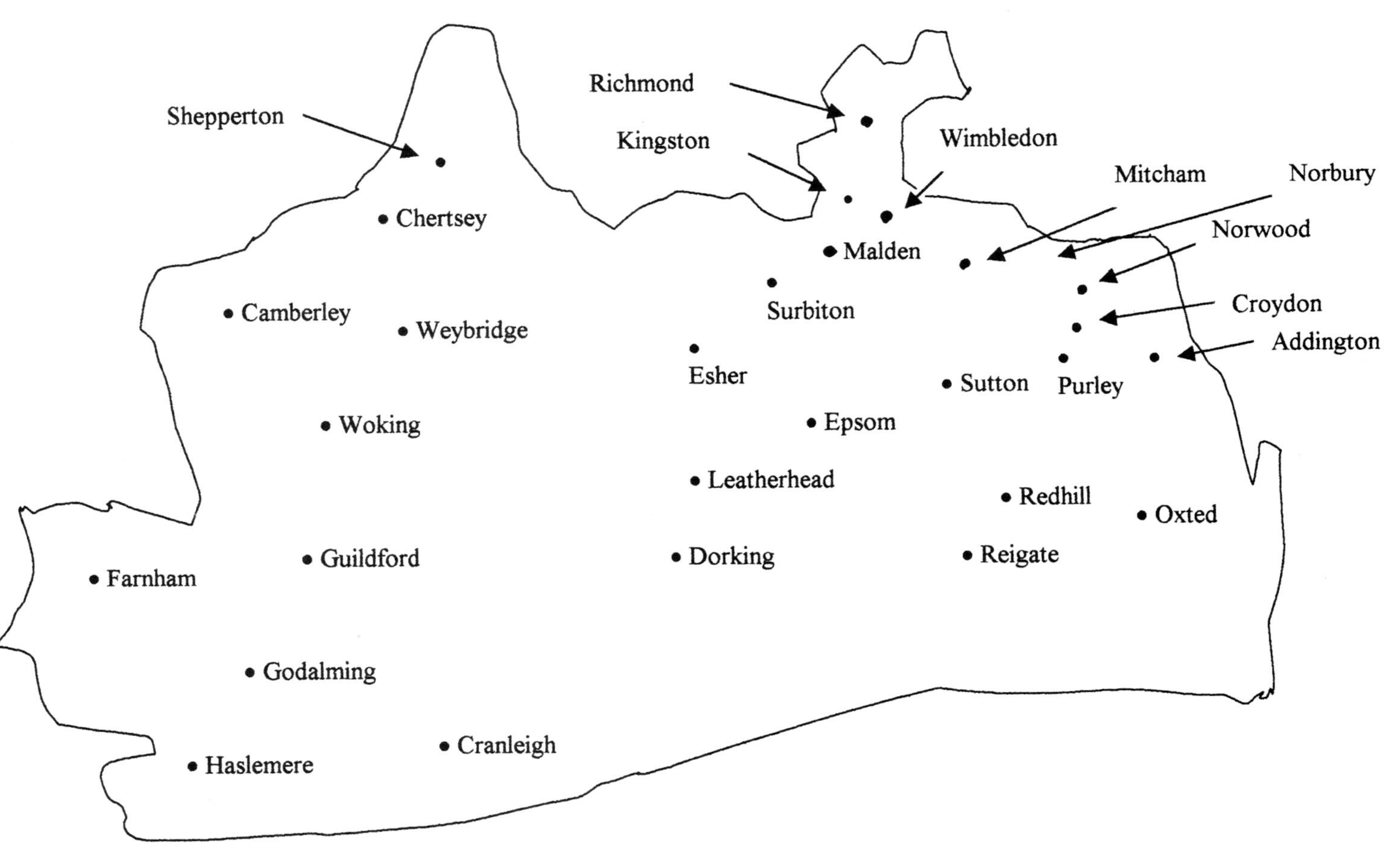


**Map showing the approximate area covered by the Surrey units, the major county towns and Battalion Headquarters.**

the Battalions were formed at the same time. Some of the larger towns, such as Richmond, Kingston and Woking, would have to wait many months before they were granted their own Battalion. This is not to say that there were no Home Guard units in these towns. Richmond was represented by a Company within the 27th County of London (Roehampton) Battalion until the formation of the 63rd Surrey (Richmond) Battalion on April 1st 1941. Kingston, meanwhile, was included within the 53rd Surrey Battalion, the 64th Surrey (Kingston) Battalion being established on May 1st 1943. Woking originally came within the 1st Surrey (Camberley) Battalion.

(The 1st, 2nd, 4th, 5th, 7th, 8th, 9th, 11th, 12th, 13th, 32nd, 33rd, 58th, 59th, 60th, 61st and 62nd Battalions were eventually to be affiliated to the Queen's Royal West Surrey Regiment; the3rd, 6th, 10th, 51st, 52nd, 53rd, 54th, 55th, 56th, 57th, 63rd and 64th Battalions were affiliated to the East Surrey Regiment.)

***Battlecraft Home Guard style as imagined by the 'Croydon Times' in 1944.***
***(Reproduced by kind permission of the Croydon Advertiser Group)***

# CHAPTER FIVE - TRAINING

## HOME ON THE RANGE

In the early days, many a volunteer utilised the ranges at Bisley for rifle and musketry practice. Bisley was never designated as a LDV/Home Guard school, being available to all who wanted to practice their shooting skills (and had the right licence etc!). The ranges at Bisley were closed for a time in late 1940 and members had to find other such locations on which to practice. (Bisley was used by the Home Guard throughout the war, Guildford members, for example, attending a Weapons Training Course there in July 1941).

Many units set up their own ranges in requisitioned properties or on land adjoining their own headquarters, this particularly being the case in the 12th (3rd Southern Railway) Battalion. A bombing range for example, was built in Knowle Park, home of Mr D Berdoe Wilkinson, for the use of members in Cranleigh.

Rifle ranges were soon established at several locations, including one at Westcott which was used by men of the 4th (Guildford) Battalion on at least two occasions, in July 1941 and September/ October 1943. The 5th Battalion established their own range at Brockham, whilst the 2nd (Farnham) Battalion used the Army's ranges at Pirbright and Ash as well as Bisley. The author Charles Graves was a member of a London Home Guard Platoon and his unit also made several visits to the range at Ash. Members in Bagshot used ranges at Sandhurst College and Blackdown and also built their own range. John Burrows remembers one particular visit to Blackdown. "My opponent and I had finished firing and I found that my target was quite unmarked, whilst that of my opponent had 10 bulls indicated. I had been firing at the wrong target!"

Derek Norris recalls that "there was a very good rifle range and assault course at Tillingdown, by the Caterham by-pass, where an evil Guards Sergeant would harass his pupils with live Vickers fire and practice grenades."

Ronald Hack remembers the Wrecclesham Home Guard's time on various practice ranges, including "the Sand-pit off Weydon Lane for rifle and Thompson MG practice. In the other direction, the Patersons Sand pit near Willey Mill was used for the Sten Guns and our own base sufficed for ·22 firing. The grenade range was some distance away on the common at Black Lake towards Tilford and was also used for practicing with our Spigot Mortars".

Accidents inevitably happened on the ranges. Ken Wicks, a member of the Redhill Home Guard remembers one particular incident during hand grenade practice, on this occasion using live grenades. "This type of practice was done standing in a 6ft deep slit trench and lobbing the grenades over the top of the trench, in an over-arm action, just like a bowler does in cricket. The first two that I threw, went perfect, it was the third grenade which I threw which nearly put paid to both the instructor and myself. I threw the grenade exactly as the first two, but some-how or other, instead of going over the top of the trench, and landing about 50-60 feet away from the trench, it went straight up in the air, and the next thing I knew, the instructor gave me one almighty shove, and I landed flat on my face, with the Instructor on top of me, then the grenade exploded, but lucky for both of us, the fuse that was used, was a 7 second one and not the 4 second fuse that was being used by the Army, as the grenade had landed about 12 inches away from the edge of the trench, and it was the quick thinking of instructor, that saved us from having our brains plastered over the sides of the trench. After picking ourselves up, the only thing the instructor said, was," that was lucky, I thought it was coming straight down into the trench," I could not say anything; I was too bloody scared by the near miss to utter a word, and shaking like a leaf In the bargain, all I could think of, was getting out of the trench. Needless to say, it was a long time before I was allowed to live it down, by the other men, although the ribbing was done in a good-natured way, as most of them had seen service during the

First World War. That is one experience I would never want to go through again believe me. I still get cold shivers whenever I think of it."

Ken Molyneux's uncle in Newdigate also had an experience he would not forget. "The Platoon were practising in the Boarhill Rifle Range, where they took receipt of an EY Rifle and the practice bombs and blanks to go with it, but no instructions. Uncle volunteered to fire it and, in total ignorance, proceeded to do so in the standing position from the shoulder! He only fired it twice and you can imagine the effect!".

Training was given at Company/Platoon level by those with previous knowledge of foot drill, musketry and unarmed combat, the younger members of the LDV/Home Guard benefiting greatly from the expertise of those who had 'seen it all before'. The first course attended by LDV members in Malden was held at Battalion headquarters in June 1940, giving members instruction on various methods of bombing. A few days later, local leaders were asked to submit the names of men who could attend courses on the use of anti-tank rifles, Lewis Guns and Bren Guns, despite the fact that few of any of these weapons had been issued to the LDV as a whole.

However, it was soon found that, with more modern methods of warfare and more up to date weaponry being introduced all the time into the LDV/Home Guard, even those with previous military experience needed training in some aspects of Home Guard work.

## BACK TO SCHOOL

There were several gentlemen who, greatly impressed with the ideology behind the formation of the LDV/Home Guard, now sought to play a part in their training.

Among these concerned citizens was Tom Wintringham, a veteran of the Spanish Civil War (1936-1938) and now proprietor of the magazine 'Picture Post'. Wintringham, with the help of members of his staff who had also seen action in Spain, set up a training school at Osterley Park, in Middlesex and dedicated it to the training of the LDV/Home Guard. The school taught members all manner of tactics learnt during the fighting in Spain, including grenade throwing, manning road blocks, basic fieldcraft and methods of ambushing the enemy. Wintringham's school was very successful. It was so successful in fact that it was eventually taken over the War Office and, despite the Department's initial reluctance, given official recognition as a Home Guard training school.

Osterley would never have been capable of fully meeting the needs of all Britain's Home Guards. As the school had established a fine reputation for the way it taught its students the lessons learnt in Spain, its teaching methods now began to be copied by new schools formed right across the country. Several Home Guard schools were established in the south of England, among them ones at Amberley and Burwash. The latter school was founded by another journalist with experience of the war in Spain, Major John Langdon-Davies, formerly a reporter with 'News Chronicle'. Courses held at Burwash were specifically dedicated to teaching members the arts of fieldcraft and living off the land. Cpl L P Tupping of Cranleigh was just one Surrey Home Guard who became an 'expert' in such matters, having attended Burwash during 1943. Specialised Street Fighting Schools were also established at Eastbourne and Worthing.

The county of Surrey included several Home Guard schools within its boundaries, including ones at Denbies, Epsom and Reigate. We shall now have a brief look at the work carried out at each of these schools.

## DENBIES

The first official Home Guard school in Surrey was set up near Dorking, on land that is now part of the county's most successful vineyard and wine producing area. Denbies Home Guard School, officially designated as No.1 Home Guard School, was established in October 1940 and, although training originally centred on fieldcraft and drill, the instruction given there later also covered all aspects of Home Guard weaponry. Chalk pits within the school's boundaries were used to test weapons such as the Northover Projector and grenade throwing pits were constructed so as to enable members to practice with live ammunition, unfortunately leading to a few casualties. Several thousand Home Guards were to pass through Denbies, including many members from outside the county of Surrey.

Among those to visit the school was Lt Col N H H Ralston of the 51st Battalion who attended an Officer's Course there during April 1942. Lt Col Redfern, Commanding Officer of the 63rd (Richmond) Battalion, attended two Officer's courses at the school during 1941 in addition to courses held by the Welsh Guards at their base at Sandown Park.

Denbies also operated a Travelling Wing which visited many Battalions to give members training in their home areas. One of the villages visited by the Travelling Wing was Cranleigh, Officers and NCOs there receiving an "intensive two day course" during 1941. The Wing was very successful and did not limit its operations to Surrey Battalions, visiting the Sussex towns of Worthing and Chichester during September 1942.

## EPSOM

The training school at Epsom was set up in the main grandstand of the racecourse famous for its annual staging of the Derby. Opened on June 21st 1941 by the GOC London District, Lt Gen Sir Sergison Brooke KCB in the company of the Rt Hon Clement Attlee the school was established by W Zone, the 56th Battalion providing a large number of the instructors and administrators who manned the school. Thirteen weekend courses were held at the racecourse during the summer of 1941, giving members instruction on subjects such as drill, grenade throwing and combating an enemy, as well as the use of various Home Guard weaponry. The school was under the command of Col A G Bartholomew, who was then a Private in the 56th (Epsom) Battalion.

## REIGATE FIELDCRAFT SCHOOL (BETCHWORTH GOLF COURSE/BUCKLAND)

"Somewhere in Surrey" ran a typical newspaper report in September 1941, "a disused and overgrown golf course is playing its part in putting a spoke into Hitler's wheel. During the week its sole occupants are sheep who graze undisturbed by anything more than a few people who use the footpath across the course; but at the week-end the sheep are co-tenants with members of the Home Guard from all parts of Surrey who come to learn the art of camouflage, stalking, observing and sniping in a Fieldcraft School which is being run under the auspices of the 8th Surrey (Reigate) Battalion Home Guard."

The writer of this article, a reporter from the Surrey Mirror and County Post, had been invited to attend the school on Sunday August 31st 1941. On the same day the school received a visit from the Lord Lieutenant of Surrey, Sir Malcolm Fraser in the company of Officers of the 8th Battalion.

The reporter was impressed with what he saw. "A more ideal setting for such a school could hardly be imagined" he wrote. "There are clumps of woodland, wide open spaces, slopes and valleys, 'folds' in rising ground, a pond, a brook and an appreciable amount of barbed wire."

The Betchworth School was commanded by Lt W R Howe Pringle, the instructors having themselves been trained at various Home Guard schools, including the ones at Burwash, Amberley and Denbies.

The visitors to Betchworth that August day were treated to a full demonstration of the work carried out at the school. This included listening into a lecture on various aspects of camouflage. This lecture was given by Mr Gausden, the Art Director of the Gaumont British Picture Corporation, a gentleman considered very important to the succssful running of the school. "A practical demonstration followed, the students turning round to inspect the bracken and bushes bordering the field. A helmet with nothing but the ordinary paint camouflage was easily visible as its owner crouched behind the bracken. We were invited to spot two more snipers hidden in the undergrowth, but not until the second raised a hand in response to Lt Pringle's call were we able to locate him. Even so, cleverly as he was concealed, this man had committed a fault in that he would have had to fire through cover instead of around it. At another call from Lt Pringle, the third man, correctly placed to have wiped out the entire party, arose almost on our left flank, until then he had been completely invisible."

Further demonstrations on the wisdom of good camouflaging followed. Asked to locate six snipers, the party failed to spot three of them and only located the other three with a good deal of help from Lt Pringle. The sniping party was photographed with Sir Malcolm Fraser, the Lord Lieutenant commenting that if the snipers "failed to appear in the photograph it would be added proof of the effectiveness of their dress!"

After lunch the visitors listened to a lecture on how to move silently through wooded countryside whilst carrying various items of equipment. Some of the students were then asked to assume the role of paratroopers who had occupied a wood. They were then told that the wood was being shelled and that they needed to break out using available cover and remembering all they had learnt about effective camouflage. Suitably camouflaged Home Guard 'snipers' would track their every move and attempt to stop them getting out. Only two of the 'paratroopers' broke free (two others coming close), the snipers keeping themselves well hidden throughout the exercise.

The afternoon's work finished, the reporter left the camp. "A glance at the camp time schedule for the two days would convince the most hardened sceptic that 'camp' is no synonym for week-end holiday; this camp, or school, stands for darned hard work, and that so many Home Guards volunteer for this strenuous course is surely proof enough that they are heart and soul in the task that one day may fall to them.

The Home Guard is very conscious of its role should invasion come and is willing, in fact enthusiastic, to learn everything they can to make an invader's lot thoroughly unpleasant."

Those attending the school found themselves with a very full weekend. A typical Saturday and Sunday would see the 'students' arriving by 4pm on the Saturday, working through to nearly midnight on the first day. They would then be woken at 6.30am on the Sunday, an inspection of rifles being the first event of the day. Instruction on unarmed combat would be given before breakfast, which was taken at about 8.30am. The rest of Sunday would be fully taken up with various talks and demonstrations, not a minute being wasted. Mr Gausden would give his lecture on camouflage at about 11am, members practising stalking tactics in the middle of the afternoon. The course would be finally dismissed at about 8pm on the Sunday night.

The School continued at Betchworth throughout 1941 and 1942, 33 weekend courses being held during this time. Amongst those attending the courses were members of the 3rd, 7th and 8th Surrey Battalions along with several from London and Kent. The school later moved to 'Shagbrook' on the Dorking Road through Buckland, finding a new home on land adjoining Reigate Heath.

Many other 'schools' were set up by a variety of Companies and Battalions in Surrey, among them one at Cherfold Stable, Ramsnest, used in the winter of 1943 by members of B Company, 5th (Cranleigh/Bramley) Battalion.

Schools were also established by the Southern Railway, at Gomshall, and the GPO at Brighton and Guildford. These schools will be looked at within the relevant sections of the chapter 'The Specialists' later in the book.

## TRAINING MANUALS

Several publications were available to assist Home Guards in their training, although not all of them were officially approved by the War Office.

Individual booklets were available on all aspects of Home Guard work from signalling, map reading and camouflage through to street fighting and house clearance. Some publications attempted to cover all the Home Guard's duties in one go. Manuals were also issued for many of the weapons used by the Home Guard. Examples of this type of booklet are 'The Complete Lewis Gunner' and 'The Browning Heavy Machine Gun Mechanism Made Easy'.

The War Office issued their own instruction manuals covering subjects such as drill and protection against gas. Perhaps the most comprehensive set of manuals produced by the War Office began to appear in 1942. Entitled "Home Guard Instructions No. 51, Battlecraft and Battle Drill For The Home Guard" (Parts I to IV) the manuals dealt with (Part I) the use of live ammunition, night training and leadership, (Part II) the Battle Platoon, (Part III) fighting patrols and patrolling built up areas and (Part IV) the organisation of defence, road blocks and drills for town fighting.

The War Office also issued Instruction Circulars to the Battalions, including, for example, details as to exactly what was expected to be undertaken in the way of Winter Training (Instruction No. 14 – 1940). One Instruction Circular (No.15 – 1940) even gave the English equivalent of 'common

German military expressions', such as hande hoch (hands up), ergebt euch (surrender) and kommt zuruck (come back)! The circular also gave the reader an idea of how to pronounce each of the German phrases, qualifying this by saying that the exact pronunciations could 'only be learned from a German speaker'. Information Circulars were also sent to local leaders, these including details on such matters as grants for Home Guard bands (Information Circular No.1 – April 1941).

## ON FILM

To supplement the manuals, training films were made available to Battalions, including ones entitled 'Observation and Reporting', 'Name, Rank and Number – Interrogation of Prisoners of War', 'Know Your Enemy – German Airborne Troops and Equipment (Landing in Crete)', 'March Discipline' and 'Elementary Map Reading – Know Your Way'. These films and many more could be hired out to Battalions as and when required, but they were also shown by the War Office's Travelling Wing and by the Southern Railway through the use of its Cinema Coach (See section on the Southern Railway's Home Guard). Projectors could also be hired out if one was not available to a unit requesting one of the films.

War Office instructional films were not the only ones to be seen by the Home Guard. In Lightwater, for example, the local Home Guards were shown Ministry of Information films and Will Hay comedies in a bid to raise funds for a new HQ for the village's Platoon. Film was also used to 'advertise' the presence of the Home Guard, the Ewhurst Women's Institute being shown a film of the village's Platoon arriving on duty during the summer of 1942. Private A E Low of the 58th Battalion, meanwhile, made a film about his Battalion and its activities during 1943. The film, described as a 'splendid piece of work' was shown throughout the Battalion as well as to member's friends and relatives.

## ON EXERCISE

Apart from the capture of a few German airmen, the Home Guard were to have little face to face contact with the enemy but still had to be prepared to meet all eventualities. As a result, Home Guard units regularly participated in training exercises to keep the men on their toes. These were often held in conjunction with locally based regular troops, or perhaps with other local Home Guard units or Civil Defence bodies.

Derek Norris can recall one particular event in the life of the Purley Mobile Column. "I remember one particular weekend exercise with the Guards in 1942. Their objective was to take Croydon Airport, ours to harass them before they reached it.

We marched off from our parade ground at Purley Cricket Club in a fierce thunderstorm, the rain coming down like stair rods and the sky illuminated every few seconds by lightening. We deployed across the fields on Meadow Hill and lay in the wet grass for the enemy to come from the direction of the Golf Course. After a few hours of this misery we withdrew (I never found out why) to stand huddled against the hedges in Woodcote Grove Road at the comer of Meadow Hill opposite Woodcote Green.

The storm passed and all was quiet. Suddenly, we heard a low whirring swishing sound and the padding of feet and round the comer from Meadow Hill there appeared in the darkness Army trucks and jogging men keeping pace. With blackened faces, lightly dressed in commando hats, soft shoes and rifles taped to deaden noise, we could hardly see or hear them. I cannot now remember our Commander's name but I do remember him shouting in his Scottish accent 'Up the Mobile!'.

We all surged into the road, hobnails crunching, gas capes crackling and rifle slings clattering. Then followed a splendid show of pyrotechnics and I still wonder what the occupants of the adjoining houses must have thought. The house on the comer did not have a brick wall in those days and the battle spilled over into the garden. I dread to think what happened to the vegetable patch!

I believe the outcome was quite successful. Although the Mobile Column (according to the umpires) ceased to exist after the affray, the Guards did not get everything their own way. Apparently, by the time they reached the airport perimeter they were so broken up they were easily dealt with by the RAF and other Regulars."

In Woking the Home Guards fought a 'battle' at Mizens Farm, Horsell. Held in conjunction with British Canadian, Polish, and Free French troops, the exercise was probably the largest carried out in the Woking area and involved just about every Platoon in the 11th Battalion. Dennis Batten took part in the exercise. "We left our H.Q. at 6pm" he later recalled "and we then marched down to the six crossroads and into the woods. Our 'target' was to reach Fairoaks airfield. This we achieved but not before getting soaked in crossing the Mimbridge stream and lost somewhere out on the common. Once at the airfield things didn't go too well. All of the men were tired, wet and hungry, and wanted nothing more than to sit down under cover for a well earned 'brew up'. The officer commanding Fairoaks wouldn't allow the Naafi tea room to be opened. This made the boys really angry and for a time it looked like a small riot would break out. Eventually we got our tea, and then left the airfield and crossed over the fields into the buildings of Mizens Farm. Here we came under mortar attack, next thing we knew we were being assaulted by Polish manned Bren carriers. Some of the chaps (me included) took up positions in one of the farm buildings, giving us a good vantage point and we were able to fire on the "enemy" without being seen. Our platoon put one carrier out of action by dropping a "clay bomb"(practice grenade)on it, this badly damaged the radio equipment! Don't think the crew were hurt, just a little shaken up. All in all it was a good night and taught us some important lessons". Another participant who remembers that night in the summer of 1941 is Mr. H. Mizen, a member of the family who owned the farm for many years, and then a volunteer in one of the Horsell platoons. "It was a star-lit evening and a little chilly, everything was suddenly disrupted by the sound of explosions and automatic weapons fire. I can remember looking up from by prone position and seeing armoured vehicles whizzing along with their guns blazing, it was all very confusing and at the same time very exciting. The battle gave a real insight into warfare and I'm glad that we never had to face the real thing!"

Ray Lowther was a member of the Chertsey Home Guard and remembers several exercises held by his Platoon. "We had exercises with units of the Canadian Army stationed somewhere in the Woking district. The Canadians were a 'tough lot' and we had a good relationship with them. The only snag was that at times they used live ammunition. I recall on one occasion we had to crawl along a sandpit on St Ann's Hill, Chertsey with the Canadians having two Bren or machine guns with instructions to fire about 18 inches over our heads. It was quite a lengthy crawl and from out of the corners of our eyes we could see the bullets hitting the sand around six inches in front or above our heads.

On another occasion, the exercise was in fields around Laleham Golf Course (Middlesex). One, presumably tired, Canadian saw some golfers standing in front of a corrugated iron shed and although some distance away, he decided to brighten proceedings. He let fly with three bullets, which, judging by the jumping around and urgent scattering of the golfers, must have made quite a noise when they struck the shed. (Of course we were lucky to have the Canadians on our side during the War).

One weekend we held an exercise near Chertsey Cemetery when I was a member of a Platoon guarding a railway footbridge. The main route to this was along a lane which passed the cemetery. At one point some undertakers drew up in a hearse and they were allowed to pass along the lane through the guard. They left the hearse and shouldered a coffin but, instead of having a body in it, the undertakers (part of the enemy force) had filled it with rifles and grenades. At the time I was a reporter on the 'Surrey Herald' and I was able on the Monday morning to take into the paper a 'par' in which I made a corny reference to them 'carrying their deadly load'. Subsequently it hit the national press!".

Some exercises were held to test specific aspects of Home Guard activity. The weekend of August 30th/31st 1942 saw the 62nd (Norbury) Battalion engaged in a 24 hour Zone exercise. All the other Battalions in Z Zone, including the 32nd, 33rd, 58th, 59th, 60th and 61st Surrey Battalions took part alongside a large number of regular troops. The exercise was mainly arranged to test Home Guard feeding arrangements, including how the Battalions would provide meals for their men during a 24 hour period of duty.

A number of Nodal Point exercises were held in Cranleigh. These included one during which a coffin and its bearers was allowed to pass through a defended area, members of the Home Guard even saluting the coffin on its way!. They were not too pleased when the deceased came to life and it was proved that the Home Guard's defences had been breached.

Exercises sometimes failed to go too smoothly for quite justifiable reasons. One exercise in Cranleigh, held by E Company , 5th Battalion in conjunction with the village's Civil Defence services, was 'spoilt' when the RAF failed to turn up to drop some dummy bombs. "The RAF was of course better engaged elsewhere but had had no time to inform us", was the comment made in E Company's official history. The situation was a bit different in Wrecclesham, where one 'attack' was "given away by a passing cat making a lot of noise and alerting the sentries".

The Surrey Advertiser carried several reports of Home Guard exercises held during 1942. On November 7th, the paper carried a report on an exercise in Bagshot on the previous Sunday involving units from Bagshot, Windlesham, Lightwater and Sunningdale. The edition of December 26th gave readers details of a similar exercise held in Haslemere on December 20th. Another report, entitled 'Who won the Battle of Godalming' appeared in the paper on November 21st 1942.

Local newspapers also gave 'warnings' to the public if any disruption was likely to be caused as a result of any planned manoeuvres. Sunday December 13th saw a large scale exercise being carried out by members of Home Guard Platoons from Milford, Elstead, Shackleford, Compton, Puttenham, Tilford and Seale alongside local Civil Defence Services. 'Normal quietude on Sunday likely to be disturbed tomorrow, exercise in morning. The public asked to co-operate by carrying out orders from those in authority', read the Surrey Advertiser of December 12th.

John Burrows was a dispatch rider with the Bagshot Home Guard and was often used to take messages to headquarters or between platoon headquarters and to men on exercise. Other exercises involved members' relatives to test the Home Guard's defences. Mrs Pickering remembers that "on one exercise I was 'conscripted' to get a platform ticket at the railway station and walk along the line to see if the pill box at the junction was occupied by the 'enemy'. On another occasion I and another young girl took the arms of one of the younger Home Guard members, so that he looked like a soldier on leave, and walk into enemy territory to gain intelligence. We succeeded."

Some exercises became a bit too much like the real thing. In Guildford, Private James Fisher was amongst some men detailed to advance from Stoke Park through to the village of Burpham. Whilst on all fours, approaching a bush just off the main Dorking road Pte Fisher was surprised to be fired upon by men travelling in a lorry. He was further surprised to find out later that the shots were not fired by Burpham Home Guards but were fired in earnest by a group of Canadian regulars who were stationed locally. Apparently a prisoner of war had escaped from custody and the Canadians had mistaken Private Fisher for their quarry.

This incident occurred during one of the many Home Guard exercises held in the Guildford area during the war. Several full scale exercises were held in the town during 1942, notably over the weekend of May 16th/17th, the occasion of the Home Guard's 2nd birthday. In order to test the Home Guard's ability to defend Guildford, a paratroop landing was simulated on Sunday May 17th, the 'invaders' swiftly moving towards the town. The Home Guard was called out and, although the town's defences were breached within four hours, it was evident that the Home Guard would have caused the attackers to suffer many casualties and much delay. The local military Commander said afterwards that he hoped "that those who watched the progress of this exercise will realise that the Home Guard, forming the bulk of the garrison, were being put to a very high test of efficiency and that they have come through it with remarkable credit to everyone from their Commanding Officer down. We have put everyone through it. We have introduced as far as we possibly could the atmosphere of war, with casualties, bombing and everything unpleasant (except gas) that we could think of which would disrupt the controls, yet Guildford has stood up to it very well."

On December 5th 1943 a further exercise in the town was attended by the GOC Home forces, whilst the biggest 'action stations' exercise undertaken by the 4th Battalion was held during March 1944 . The following June saw members take part in the 'Battle of Guildford' as part of the town's Salute the Soldier week.

## HOME GUARD TRAINING FORTNIGHT

In November 1941 Lieutenant General B L Montgomery was appointed GOC South-Eastern

Command. The newly appointed Montgomery immediately made plans to strengthen the Home Forces now under his command, part of those plans being to improve the capability of the Home Guard. In March 1942 he announced that the period June 6th to 21st would be given up to Home Guard training. For those two weeks regular troops based in the South East would be detailed to train the Home Guards in their area. Despite the potentially busy time of year and the lack of any significant leisure time to themselves, all Home Guards were encouraged to take any holiday due to them during that fortnight so that they could attend the training sessions. All Home Guard training schools were closed during those two weeks.

In many areas the task of training the Home Guards fell to Canadian troops. The 4th Surrey (Guildford) Battalion were affiliated to the Toronto Scottish Battalion during this period. Each Company within the Battalion took part in one night exercise in each of the two weeks and large scale Battalion exercises were held over the weekends of June 13/14th and 20/21st. The Canadians were able to give the Guildfordians the benefit of their experience as machine gun experts. A Platoon of the Toronto Scottish also undertook the training of Cranleigh's Home Guards. Training here was concentrated on battle drill and covered such aspects as street fighting and clearing a wood.

The 8th Reconnaissance (Recce) Battalion of the 2nd Canadian Division, Canadian Expeditionary Force took the 8th Battalion under their wing for the two week training session. Described by the Battalion's historian as 'tough in the extreme', the fortnight again mainly covered field operations and the organisation of a unit as a fighting force. A full scale exercise was held at the end of the second weekend, which included live ammunition being fired 'at' the Home Guards.

The Home Guard Training Fortnight was a great success. In some areas 90% of Home Guards turned out during the two week period and on June 27th Montgomery wrote to the Battalions to thank the men for their efforts. Montgomery was particularly mindful of the relationships that had been built up between regular troops and the Home Guards saying that "the contacts that have been established during the fortnight have created a feeling of mutual respect and comradeship between Home Guard and Army units. This will prove of the greatest value should we be called upon to defeat an attempted invasion of our country. I congratulate all concerned, both Home Guard and Army on the successful results of the Home Guard Fortnight in the South East".

## CAMPS

Many Battalions/Companies decided that one the best ways to give their men a period of concentrated training was to take them away for weekend camps.

The 63rd Battalion's first camp was held in Richmond Park during May 1943. Some 400 Home Guards were expected, although 500 were actually catered for. In the event 800 turned up. This was not the first camp held in Richmond Park; 600 members of the 51st Battalion had attended a weekend camp there during July 1941.

One camp, held in July 1944 by D Company 4th Battalion in Hascombe, was to be disrupted somewhat, though, when the Company Commander, Major Bevan, met with a 'serious accident' whilst setting booby traps for his men, necessitating a visit to the local hospital.

## HOME GUARD PROFICIENCY TESTS

One of the ways chosen to recognise the level of efficiency attained by each individual Home Guard was through the awarding of Proficiency Badges.

Testing was introduced by the War Office in April 1941, high ranking Home Guards and occasionally regular Army Officers adjudicating whether a sufficiently high standard had been reached in a number of subjects. Those passing the tests, which included general knowledge (relating to the Home Guard) and the use of a rifle together with at least one other subject, were awarded a certificate and, if below the rank of Sergeant, were entitled to wear a Proficiency Badge on the lower right sleeve of their battledress blouse.

These tests were a valuable means of assessing the suitability of candidates for promotion. So much so that in November 1943 it was decided in many areas that promotion would not be given to any man who had not yet passed the tests. Furthermore, if any NCO had not qualified for his badge by March 1st 1944, Commanding Officers would be asked to seriously consider whether the man should be retained in his rank. No such pressure was put on those of officer status but they were expected to pass the tests as an example to their men.

In Guildford, the Battalion historian recalls that the tests were deliberately set at a higher standard. This does not seem to have deterred too many members from taking the tests however and in March 1944 the historian was pleased to note that many candidates had obtained their second badge.

Although it was by no means compulsory for members to go through the testing procedure, large numbers of Home Guards did so and a high percentage passed to the required standard. Between 1941 and 1944, for example, 955 members of the 58th (Purley) Battalion were to be successful in the tests, this number being approximately 30% of the total number of members who eventually passed through the Battalion.

***Members of the LDV being given instruction on the use of the P17 rifle at Bisley. (IWM)***

*Members of Woking's WESCo Platoon crossing the Basingstoke Canal near Spantons Wharf using a toggle rope bridge. This type of bridge would have been used if the town's canal bridges had been destroyed during an attack. (Andy Stevens)*

*Members of the Richmond Home Guard on exercise, May 2nd 1942. Some of the Battalion donned German uniforms to add a touch of realism to the proceedings. (IWM)*

# CHAPTER SIX - CONSOLIDATION

## COMMISSIONS

Commissions were never granted to the LDV, nor for a while to the Home Guard. As a result of this, LDV / Home Guard leaders were not at first permitted to wear the normal badges of rank worn by regular Army Officers. However, once the issue of denims had begun, blue cloth stripes were issued to commanders as a means of identifying their status. These strips of cloth were worn on the shoulders, 3 stripes signifying a Battalion Commander, 2 stripes a Company Commander and 1 stripe a Platoon Commander.

In the early days, those in positions of authority within the early LDV/Home Guard command structure were given no official rank. Indeed, even those at the lower end of the hierarchy were not known at first as Privates, each man merely being recognised as a "Volunteer". In February 1941, however, it was announced that commissions were to be granted to the Home Guard and for the first time the leaders were granted official rank. This did not mean that Home Guard commanders held any official position within the regular Army and in the normal course of events they could not officially give any orders or instructions to regular troops.

The first Home Guard commissions were officially published in May 1941. From this point in time, a Home Guard Battalion would be under the command of a Lieutenant Colonel, a Company Commander would usually be a Major and the man in charge of a Platoon would be a Lieutenant. The Second in Command of each unit would usually be a man one rank lower than his Commanding Officer. Therefore, the Second in Command of a Battalion would normally be a Major while the Second in Command of a Company would usually be a Captain. A 2nd Lieutenant would usually be the number two in a Platoon and would have command of a Section. All other Battalion Home Guards were now officially Privates.

A good example of the command structure leading down to a typical can be found if one looks at the set up of the 2nd Surrey (Farnham) Battalion and the Wrecclesham Platoon.

2nd Surrey (Farnham) Battalion:
Battalion Commanding Officer – Lt Col A F Hunt DSO OBE
'A' Company:-
Company Commanding Officer - Major Patrick
Company 2nd in Command Captain Townsend
No. 1. Platoon, Wrecclesham:-
Platoon Commanding Officer - Lt Koebel
Platoon 2nd in Command - 2nd Lt T Lawrence

It is perhaps worth looking at the former military ranks of the above gentlemen. Major Patrick had also held the rank of Major with the regular Army, Captain Townsend was also a retired Army Major, whilst Lt Koebel had held the rank of Colonel and was a former Commandant of the Small Arms School, Indian Army. 2nd Lieutenant Lawrence was a former member of the Gordon Highlanders and had also previously held the rank of Colonel. Other Officers and NCOs in the Battalion included Lt Mather, an ex-Admiral and Sergeant Ralph, formerly a Major with the Royal Scots Guards.

The insignia worn by Home Guard Officers and NCOs were identical to those of the regular army. A Lieutenant Colonel wore a crown and a star on each shoulder, a Major one crown on each shoulder and a Lieutenant two stars. NCOs wore stripes on each arm of their battle-dress, a Sergeant three stripes, a Corporal two and a Lance Corporal one.

## A QUESTION OF AGE

When first formed, the LDV was supposed to be open only to men between the ages of 17 and 65. As has been seen this was open to some abuse as youngsters of 14 and men of 70 plus also offered their services. In those days a blind eye was turned as, providing the volunteer was physically fit, any offer of help was gratefully accepted. In some Battalions special sections of their younger fitter men were formed.

Reminders were issued from time to time that members were expected to drop out on reaching 65. However as the force became more military minded, stricter rules were drawn up to ensure that older men were not retained. In November 1941 Battalions were advised that all officers had to retire on reaching the age of 65. Additionally all Officers already over the age of 65 had to retire by March 31st the following year. It was also announced that volunteers over the age of 65 would not normally be allowed to stay in the Home Guard although they could be retained if their Commander so wished, subject to six-monthly reports being made on their continued suitability.

The more rigidly enforced age regulations were just one of the reasons why, by the end of 1941, membership of the Home Guard had started to decline.

## MAKING UP THE NUMBERS

The turnover of Home Guard members was always quite high. Some units recorded more than twice as many having enrolled as were still in the Home Guard when it was stood down in 1944. Members had several reasons for leaving, although, as will be seen, after February 1942 resignation was not an option, unless the member had an extremely valid 'excuse'.

The roll of those leaving the Limpsfield Platoon makes interesting reading and includes:

| | |
|---|---|
| G Ashton | Transferred to 32nd Kent (Edenbridge) Battalion Home Guard, April 1943 |
| P Baillee | Resigned February 1942 to work in Civil Defence |
| L V Braysher | Resigned, to work in the Coal Mines, August 1944 (presumably as one of the conscripted Bevin Boys) |
| N E Bunn | Resigned October 1940 to join the Army |
| G A C Caton | Resigned July 1942 to join the RAF |
| K A Habgood | Resigned May 1942 to join the Royal Navy |

As can be seen, a lot of the so-called resignations from the Home Guard were due to members being called up to serve in the regular forces, although some were also transferred to other Home Guard units. Other existing nominal rolls show a variety of reasons for members leaving, among them 'medically unfit', 'surplus to requirements' and, in the case of J Owen, a member of the 62nd (Norbury) Batallion, being 'under age'.

Volunteers continued to offer their services to the Home Guard, new members coming to the force from a wide variety of backgrounds and occupations. Dr William F Wheeler served in the Farncombe Platoon between 1942 and 1944. "I was a student at St Thomas's Hospital Medical School, which was evacuated to the Godalming-Farncombe-Milford (Hydestyle) area. At the time the pre-medical and pre-clinical year students (of which I was one) were accommodated at the Manor House near Charterhouse School (whose laboratories we used as well as those arranged by the Hospital). Since we were exempt from military service as long as we maintained a good academic level, we either joined the Home Guard or ARP. I was in the Farncombe Platoon; other students (we were all male) joined the Godalming or Compton units." Joseph Ascher was a teacher with the Wandsworth School, which had been evacuated to the Woking area on the outbreak of war. He joined the Home Guard Platoon based in the nearby village of Horsell. His son, Maurice Ascher, remembers that his father "did not accept any promoted rank because the teachers also had a responsibility to their evacuated charges. However, many teachers ignored this advice. How they would have decided the tug of war between Home Guard duties and protection of the school children evacuated from their parents was, of course, never tested."

Many of the Home Guard's younger members went on to give equally valuable service in the regular forces during the Second World War. John Lyons was one such member of the LDV / Home Guard. "In 1941 I volunteered and was accepted for air crew duties. I joined a Lancaster crew as a rear gunner with 83 Pathfinder Squadron at Wyton, taking part in the raids on the rocket base at Peenemunde. Our losses were heavy at the period of the war an average of between 5 and 10 per cent each raid, but I survived until the end of the year taking part in half a dozen raids on Berlin. I then spent several months in hospital after we were shot down on December 22nd 1943."

Members of the 58th Battalion were pleasantly surprised to find a former member of their Battalion had been involved in a dramatic naval 'engagement' in January 1943. Rodney Dove had enrolled in June 1940,leaving the unit in December 1941 to join the Royal Navy. On January 3rd 1943, Dove took part in a 'human torpedo' operation in Palermo harbour, Sicily, leading to the sinking of the Italian Light Cruiser 'Ulpio Traiano'. Dove was awarded the DSO for his part in the action, although he was to spend the rest of the war in a German prisoner of war camp.

Redhill volunteer Ken Wicks's father and two brothers also served in the Home Guard. Whilst Mr Wicks senior had seen service during the First World War, his three sons all went on to join the Merchant Navy during the Second World War.

According to former Home Guard member John Burrows, one of the Bagshot Platoon was John Ellerman, head of the Ellerman Lines group of shipping companies who had evacuated parts of their business to Surrey. Mr Burrows remembers that "Ellerman did not really look the part of a soldier. His gaiters were invariably the wrong way round and his cap was just placed squarely on his head instead of to one side in the correct manner. To look at him and Mr Pratt, his assistant, one would have thought that Mr Pratt was the master out of the two of them. Another of his assistants was a Mr Brady. He looked as though he had just jumped into his uniform from under the mattress. However, although Mr Ellerman rarely attended parades he always took his turn on duty but rarely spoke to the other men in the Platoon".

Like many other businesses, Ellerman's were to suffer great losses during the war, including two key premises in the City of London to German bombs. However, the most tragic loss to befall the group, and quite possibly the nation, occurred at 10pm on Tuesday September 17th 1940 when the 'City of Benares' was carrying children from Liverpool to Montreal where they could grow up in a safer environment, this being arranged under a government scheme called 'Seavac'. More than 250 passengers and crew were to die as a result of this sinking, 73 of them children. 'Ellermans' though, continued to do sterling work during the war playing a very large part in the ball-bearing runs from Sweden to England, thus transporting an essential basic component of military vehicles to this country.

Cartoonist Carl Giles, known to millions of readers simply as 'Giles', was working on the 'Reynolds News' when the Home Guard was first formed. Enrolling in a Platoon in the Finchley area, Giles rose to the rank of Corporal before going off to war with his new employers, the Daily Express. Giles, News Editor at 'Reynolds News' had been Arnold Russell, a member of the Richmond Home Guard. Giles later drew a cartoon of a rather miserable lookng Russsell on duty in a churchyard whilst wearing his Home Guard uniform.

## CONSCRIPTION

In December 1941, the government introduced the National Service (No.2) Act which made it compulsorily for all adults to perform some kind of national service in support of the country's war effort. One of the provisions of the bill was that all males between the ages of 18 and 51 were liable to be called on for service with the Home Guard, in an attempt to bring certain Battalions up to their required strength. All members of the Home Guard were required to perform a maximum 48 hours training or patrols a month. Anyone failing to do their full quota of hours, if called upon, was liable to be fined £10 or could even face a month in jail. It was emphasised that the figure of 48 hours a month was the maximum expected of a Home Guard and not the minimum and unit commanders were expected to take into account a member's circumstances, such as employment, when allocating duties. Additionally members were now unable to leave the force until they reached the age of 65 although existing members could resign from the force before February 16th 1942 if they did not want to continue in the Home Guard. However those who did resign were liable to be re-directed back into the Home Guard if they were below the age of 51.

Whilst some members did resign, membership of the Home Guard increased during the first 6 months of 1942. In December 1941 1,530,000 men belonged to the Home Guard but by the following March this figure had increased to 1,793,000.

Although the relationship between the original volunteers and those recently directed to the Home Guard could have been an awkward one, compulsory membership of the Home Guard caused the Battalions little problems. In Sutton it was noted that many of those conscripted commented later how they wished they had joined the Home Guard "much sooner".

For all the good compulsion did, though, the direction of men to the Home Guard changed the nature of the force forever. Now a highly trained body of men, the Home Guard was no longer the volunteer army of 1940.

## THE VILLAGE HOME GUARD

The Home Guard was set up in such a way that the units in small villages were the last in a long chain that stretched all the way down from the War Office. A typical such Platoon was established in the village of Ewhurst.

There were 2 Platoons based in Ewhurst, both being part of F Company 5th Surrey (Bramley) Battalion Home Guard. No.55 Platoon was based at Ewhurst Place and was formed by members of Lloyds Bank Executor and Trustee Department, evacuated to the area in August 29/30th 1939 (see 'A Private Concern'). No.54 Platoon meanwhile was formed by local villagers and had its headquarters at a village pub, the Bulls Head. The members of No.54 Platoon came from a variety of occupations. There were, amongst others, painters, gardeners, carpenters, farmers and smallholders in the Platoon. Bill Taylor ran his own cattle haulage business, Billy Day had a grocery shop in Ockley Road, Den Ledger was a smallholder in Plough Lane and Bill Smith was a gardener whilst another Mr Smith had no excuse for being late on parade, being the son of the landlord of the Bulls Head. Les Weller's family had been farming in the village for many generations and he too joined the Platoon. Others to enrol included Horace Hubbard, a painter from Cranleigh School, Mr Charman, a gardener whose wife ran a tea room and draper's shop in Cranleigh Road, Mr Hume a governor of Ewhurst School who taught the boys cricket and football during the war and Harry Wilson, a butler. The unit was commanded at first by Col G Sartorius and later by Lt J E Hamshire, a baker from Gadbridge Lane. Many of these gentlemen would have had at least some military experience.

The author's grandfather, George Crook was also a gardener and enrolled in the Ewhurst Platoon on July 17th 1940. Born on July 22nd 1899 in Rushford, Norfolk, George joined the Royal Norfolk Regiment in 1917, serving in France during World War One. His brother, John also saw service in the First World War but was unfortunately to die at the age of 24 as a result of injuries sustained on the Western Front. The Home Guard certificate issued to George Crook shortly after stand down in 1944 shows that he had two spells in the force as, in October 1942, he took a brief break from gardening and went to work at a munitions factory for 14 months, returning to the Ewhurst Home Guard on December 17th 1943.

The village's Home Guard Platoon certainly seems to have played an important role in village life. On November 30th 1940 the Surrey Advertiser carried a report entitled 'Record Knitting Feat' which informed readers that the WVS had "knitted 71 helmets, 74 scarves and 66 mit-muffs for the Home Guard." At the end of 1940 villagers organised a "delightful Christmas programme of events", including an auction conducted by Richard Goulden, the BBC's Mr Pastry, raising £10 towards comforts for the village's Home Guard. Then on September 9th 1942 the Surrey Advertiser told its readers that "the Ewhurst W.I had their Annual General Meeting on September 2nd. After tea a film of events at Ewhurst was shown including the arrival of the Home Guard on duty and the arrival of evacuees in the village."

The Ewhurst Home Guard had a good relationship with other nearby units and Bill Smith's son, Alan, can still remember all night exercises being held with the Peaslake and Shere Platoons. He also recalls an event on Downhurst Meadow and target practice with the unit's Spigot Mortar. The highlight, says Alan was "brave Louis Keane pulling a target on wheels across the meadow in his truck. All good Captain Mainwaring stuff – but the Home Guard did demolish the target." Cricket matches were also held on Ewhurst Green between the village's Home Guard Platoon and the Oakwood Hill Home Guard.

## WOMEN IN THE HOME GUARD

It was not only the menfolk of Britain that wanted to play their part in the defence of their homelands. Eden's broadcast of May 14th 1940 had also appealed to many women and they too now proceeded to their local Police Station in an attempt to enrol in the new force. These attempts were somewhat in vain. No provision had been made for the enrollment of the ladies in the LDV and all were turned away, their offers of help, for the time being at least, refused.

This did not stop some women taking matters into their own hands. Guildford was one town that had seen many ladies attempting to enrol in the first few days and at least two of them joined Merrow Rifle Club to learn to shoot in case they were needed. Others were unofficially invited to join their local LDV / Home Guard units. Becky Brown undertook clerical work for the 12th Surrey (3rd Southern Railway) Battalion (see 'Specialists' section) whilst a Medical Section was raised in Malden, this being largely comprised mainly of women helpers. Originally made up of six male Home Guards, the unit was soon augmented by women who were keen to help their local unit. They were given their own special uniform and fully trained in First Aid matters. A proud boast of the 51st Battalion is that it was among the first units to train and enrol women 'members'.

Many ladies were still upset that they were unable to play a full part in the Home Guard and pressure grew on the Government to allow women to form their own defence organisations. Labour MP Dr Edith Summerskill added her voice to the arguments throughout 1940; but the authorities would not be moved.

The position was beginning to change, however. In December 1941 the National Service (No.2) Act introduced conscription for women for the first time giving those called up the choice between joining the forces or participating in war work at home, such as jobs in industry or the Land Army. Although only affecting unmarried women between the ages of 19 and 30, the act set a principle that was hard to ignore and in June 1943 the authorities finally backed down and allowed women into the previously male stronghold of the Home Guard.

The jobs the women's auxiliaries were allocated were strictly limited to non-combatant roles. A typical enrolment form would ask the applicant to choose whether they wanted to be a cook, clerk and telephonist or a driver. The ladies were also asked if they were currently engaged in any other work of national importance. Many of them were. Those volunteering to help the 59th (Addington) Battalion included Helen Pearce, a salvage steward with the WVS (Womens Voluntary Service) who also undertook fire watching duties from time to time, and Margaret Teague, then Private Secretary to the Commercial Manager of the LPTB (London Passenger Transport Board). Some of the ladies were Bank Clerks, including sisters Gwendolen and Doreen Robertson who both now volunteered for signalling (clerk and telephonist) duties with the Battalion.

Isla Franks was one of those to join this Battalion. "I was 19 years old when I became secretary of A Company of the 59th Battalion Surrey Home Guard. Our Battalion Headquarters were at Addington Palace and the Commanding Officer was Colonel H E Pearce. A Company's HQ was in Addiscombe Road, Croydon, the C/O being Major R H Shelton, DSO."

Those ladies joining the 60th (Croydon) Battalion were also asked what hours they were available to the Home Guard. Mrs Mercia McKay qualified her service a bit more, adding "the offer of my service is only to assist the O C Creed Factory Platoon Home Guard and not for any other work". Mrs McKay had been a stenographer with Creeds for 12 years.

The 33rd Battalion's enrolment form asked their prospective members to indicate which of a number of specified areas of work they were able to do, including typing, shorthand, telephone messages, book-keeping, the keeping of records, cooking and preparing of food, and driving.

The application form for membership of the 5th Battalion also included the following clauses. 'I understand that my application for and nomination to employment with the Home Guard will not exempt me from any full-time or part-time service which the Ministry of Labour & National Service may require me to undertake, nor will such nomination exempt me from performing fire prevention duty.' Secondly, 'I undertake to give my services entirely voluntarily and to perform any duties required of me at reasonable times and, in particular, to be available, if required, when the Home

Guard is mustered.'

Although the duties given to the ladies were strictly non-combat roles this did not stop them having close contact with the enemy. Isla Franks remembers one incident in Addington. "There was one occasion when a bomb fell particularly close, and the blast knocked me down HQ stairs and I hurt my leg. After that the O.C. insisted that I wear a steel helmet when the siren sounded and that I was to go into the greenhouse in the garden and wait till the raid was over, the HQ being used for storing grenades etc. This I did sitting on some sacking and resenting the time I was wasting when there was so much work to do. Eventually the all-clear sounded, and as I got up I caught the sacking and it pulled away and I found that I'd been sitting on boxes containing 60 SIP Grenades. After that I stayed in HQ, preferring to be blown up rather than fired."

Joan Johnson did not join the Home Guard but does remember spending time with her father's unit in Ewell. "Whilst waiting to go to college I became quite involved in the Home Guard. I was taught how to fire the rifle but not having any blanks available never actually fired it, which was probably fortunate. I was to threaten any parachutist whilst my mother, armed with the revolver, phoned for help. The dog and I traced the footpaths and farm tracks and later, after the concrete machine gun posts were built, we inspected them for any improper deposits. My reward was to attend the dances at the Drill Hall and dance sedately with older men in Army boots!"

No uniform was ever issued to the ladies, only a brooch made in either plastic or metal being given to those offering to help out the Battalions, this first being sanctioned on August 20th 1943. This was made very clear to those completing the enrolment forms, the one signed by those joining the 59th Battalion including the question "do you understand that no uniform will be provided." This might have caused Joan Godden a problem. "We wore trousers and old shirts until a standing order insisted that the 'Home Guard must wear government issue uniforms and no other items', which would have left us decked out in just Home Guard badges with nothing to pin them to!"

The numbers of women allowed into each Battalion at this time were strictly limited. In September 1943 Lt Col H F M Hughes, DCM, wrote to the Commander of Z Sector saying that the membership ceiling of 34 women was 'sufficient', unsurprisingly as only 5 ladies had joined the Battalion by this date.

Women were somewhat slow to join the Home Guard at first and in June 1943 only 4,000 volunteered. The 59th Battalion saw several resignations from its women auxiliaries although there were still 36 women in the Battalion in December 1944. Eighteen ladies were still with the 58th (Purley) Battalion. Despite these relatively small numbers though, 32,000 ladies were still with the Home Guard when it was stood down at the end of 1944.

***The Ewhurst Village Platoon (George Crook is in the very middle of the back row). (Ewhurst Historical Society)***

# CHAPTER SEVEN - SOCIAL AND CEREMONIAL

The very nature of the force meant that it had a large effect on day to day life in the communities it served. Although its organisation spread over the whole of Britain, the LDV/Home Guard was still very much a local affair. Its leaders were drawn from the local community, its membership often made up of a large percentage of the men-folk in the district. Whilst the Home Guard's duties were based on military necessity, one of its unofficial roles could be seen as that of boosting public confidence in the knowledge that they would be stoutly defended if ever the need arose. To achieve this end, the Home Guard had to make sure its local profile was always fairly high.

## ON PARADE

Church parades were often a favourite of the Home Guard. Many units attended services soon after their formation but a few waited several months before parading for the first time. The 'Dorking Advertiser' of July 19th 1940 carried a report on the first ceremonial parade of the town's LDVs, on Sunday July 14th. "Beribboned veterans of the last war, with a considerable sprinkling of younger men, marched smartly, maintaining perfect alignment and showing the alertness of men ready to meet any emergency". The first parade in Leatherhead was held on Sunday July 21st 1940 and was attended by Lord Ashcombe, formerly Lord Lieutenant of Surrey but now a member of the LDV. In Reigate, though, the 8th Battalion's B, C and D Companies participated in their first Church Parade as late as March 20th 1941.

Services were often held to celebrate or commemorate particular occasions. On Wednesday September 16th 1942, B Company of the 4th Battalion attended a Church parade in Stoke Church to mark the 3rd anniversary of the outbreak of war. A United Services Parade was also held at Runnymede to commemorate the occasion, this being attended by the 10th Battalion under the command of Lt Col A P Y Langhorne.

LDV/Home Guard leaders were always keen to show the progress their units had made. Things did not always go according to plan though. Bert Waugham was a member of the 11th Surrey (Woking) Battalion. One Sunday morning in the early summer of 1940 "we were marched to the Six Crossroads and told that we were to be presented to two very important persons, who would walk slowly past and watch us perform our duties. Sections were placed at ten yard intervals on the common facing the roadway. I had been trained for unarmed combat so, with the help of Charlie Brown we practised a couple of holds for them to see as they walked by, so we thought! Well, they duly arrived and to our surprise it turned out to be the late King George and General Montgomery! They started to walk down the road and when they were opposite us we started to perform and expected them to walk on. To my surprise they stood there and watched us, so I turned to Charlie to get hold of him again. However, he thought we were finished and went to hand his rifle to me, catching me under the chin. Sitting on my pants looking up at the King through a galaxy of stars I thought "King or no King, that's my lot for the moment!"

Some units forged a very close relationship with units of the regular army stationed in their area. In June 1943, Mr Vincent Massey, High Commissioner of Canada presented a field kitchen to V Sector during a parade on the Polo Ground, Roehampton. 1,200 Home Guards attended the parade to hear Mr Massey praise the force, saying "we in Canada regard it as one of the finest examples of that good citizenship which we always associate with Great Britain. The story of its growth is one of the great sagas of wartime Britain." Units represented at the parade included the 27th and 28th County of London Battalions as well as the 51st, 52nd, 53rd, 54th, 63rd and 64th Surrey Battalions. Amongst the other presentations made to the Surrey Home Guard were a couple of staff cars to the 59th Battalion by non-British members of the Bank of London and South America Ltd and a mobile canteen to F Company, 3rd (Weybridge) Battalion from the British War Relief Society's Plains Township Committee of Hudson, New York, who also donated $800 to the Company towards the canteen's upkeep.

Several Home Guards were keen to remember former colleagues who had been lost during the First World War. Many attended Remembrance Day Parades, members of the Walton on Thames Home Guard, for example, taking part in the town's parade on November 5th 1944. Members of the Eashing Home Guard, meanwhile, along with the Royal British Legion and locally based Canadian troops, attended a Remembrance Day Service at Shackleford Church on November 12th 1944.

Perhaps the best opportunities for the Home Guard to 'show off', though were the parades and displays arranged for the force's four anniversaries. The first anniversary parades were held over the weekend of May 17th and 18th 1941 although, with the war situation still being extremely uncertain, the occasion seems to have attracted little attention. Parades were also held to mark the Home Guard's 2nd anniversary. In Richmond, the Commander of V Sector, Col Sir Dudley Collins told his men that "from an unarmed and improvised beginning you have blossomed into a self-reliant and formidable force of unpaid soldiers." In Bagshot, members of several local units watched a demonstration by regular troops who showed the watching Home Guards how to storm a fortified enemy position. According to the local newspaper, this was the Home Guard's "first experience of modern warfare", although a loud speaker was present to provide a running commentary on the 'fight'. Members of the 5th Battalion, meanwhile, had a more peaceful time of it, 200 members attending a Church Parade in Peaslake.

The 3rd anniversary, though, turned into the largest celebration yet of Home Guard expertise. Instead of attending Church Parades or watching other units 'do their bit', the Home Guard chose to show members of the watching public exactly what it could do.

In Guildford, the 4th Battalion held a parade on Shalford Meadows, the men being inspected by the Lord Lieutenant of Surrey Sir Malcolm Fraser. The Battalion then went on to give a demonstration of weapons currently in its armoury, including Northover Projectors and Spigot Mortars, "engaging a tank with marked success". 3,000 watched the parade of the 51st Battalion at the University Sports Ground, Motspur Park. Spectators witnessed a parade of LDV members, all dressed in a variety of civvies and, according to the local paper, 'marching higgledy-piggledy'. The LDV were followed by a smart unit of Home Guard men led by motorcycle dispatch riders and the Battalion band, all starkly illustrating the progress made over the previous 3 years.

The 55th Battalion held their parade on Cheam Common and treated those watching to a display of just about all aspects of Home Guard work. Amongst the demonstrations given by the Battalion were ones of foot and rifle drill and bayonet fighting. Members also showed off their armoury, particularly their Northover Projectors, when in common with the 4th Battalion, they destroyed a mock-up of a German tank. The Battalion also demonstrated various aspects of battlecraft including an impressive display of members ability to effectively camouflage and conceal themselves. "The spectators were amazed when 17 men concealed on the field in front of them sprang to life at the call of an Officer; few people had been able to pick out more than one or two of them!" Displays were also given by the Battalion's motorcycle dispatch riders and one of the Battle Platoons, who put themselves through an improvised assault course "on which the obstacles were a nine foot wall, a 'river' spanned by a single rope ten feet above the ground, and two sets of barbed wire. The course was covered by 18 men, (all) with rifles and equipment, in under ten minutes".

The 33rd Battalion held a route march around Duppas Hill, Croydon and then treated spectators to a demonstration of how they would deal with an enemy gas attack. The afternoon saw a further parade through the town, this time featuring all eight Battalions within Z Sector as well as six other neighbouring Battalions. The salute was taken at Croydon Town Hall by Colonel Keevil, the Sector Commander.

The Betchworth Company of the 7th (Dorking) Battalion held their own parade at the local Golf Course, demonstrations given including ones on camouflage, night patrols and battle drill. D Company (Charlwood), meanwhile, paraded on the town's Recreation Ground, treating the watching public to a show of the members skill at bayonet fighting, unarmed combat and camouflage. This parade was attended by members of Home Guard platoons from Sidlow, Hookwood, Lowfield Heath, Farmfield, Rusper, Newdigate and Charlwood.

In Chertsey, to mark the army's successes in Tunisia, the salute was taken at the end of the parade of D Company, 10th Battalion, by a sailor who had been injured on convoy duty earlier in the war and two wounded members of the First Army.

Similar parades were also held in May 1944 to mark the Home Guard's 4th birthday.

## SPORTS

Sports events helped to keep members fit and alert. Some events even helped in members training, shooting matches, for example, giving members a good opportunity to test their ability with the rifle. One such match saw the defeat of a Godalming Platoon by members of the local Surrey Constabulary, losing by 570 points to 557. The 2nd Battalion (Farnham), meanwhile, are reported as taking part in a shooting competition at Longmoor on September 13th 1942. Inter-Company/Platoon competitions were also held from time to time. In December 1944, 29 Battalions from across the British Isles competed for the Lochboisdale Challenge Trophy. Whilst the trophy was won by the 43rd West Riding (Hatfield) Battalion, Surrey members gave a good account of themselves during the competition, 4th place being taken by the 10th Surrey (Egham and Chertsey) Battalion, the 1st Surrey (Camberley) being just behind them in 5th position. Competitions such as this one were regularly held throughout the Home Guard, some units winning several items of silverware as testimony to their prowess.

On August 23rd 1942, C Company 10th Battalion held an Athletics Meeting at Weymann's Sports Ground, Addlestone. The event was won by No.14 Platoon (85 points), No.12 Platoon (57 points) were second, No.15 Platoon (56 points) were 3rd and No.18 Platoon (55 points) 4th. The trophy was presented to the winners by Major C F Jacottet, C Company's Commanding Officer. Amongst the stars that day was Lt Morris of No. 14 Platoon, the winner of the veteran's 100 yards and the Officer's 220 yards races. The day also featured One Mile and Three Mile Cycle races, both won by Manning of No.18 Platoon.

August also saw the Home Guard try their luck at Cricket. On the 1st of the month a team from the Guildford Royal Grammar School were beaten by a Guildford Home Guard XI, losing by 26 runs. W Gardner was the hero for the Home Guard, scoring 45 as well as taking 5 RGS wickets for 24 runs.

The 51st Battalion, meanwhile offered the facilities at their Battalion HQ to members of the US Army so that they could stage a Baseball match in aid of Malden's 'Wings For Victory' appeal in 1943. A large audience is reported as having watched the day's proceedings, fascinated no doubt by a sport not often seen in Britain, despite its having been 'invented' in England many years ago. A further match due to be played in June 1944 though had to be cancelled due to V1s making several unwanted appearances in the skies over Surrey. The Battalion also had to cancel a dance and a boxing match for the same reason.

## FUND RAISING EVENTS

Perhaps the biggest fund raising events that the Home Guard were able to participate in were the War Weapons (1941), Warships (1941/42), Wings For Victory (1943) and Salute the Soldier weeks (1944). Promoted in villages, towns and cities across the country the campaigns gave the 'ordinary person' the chance to feel that they were doing something material to support the war effort. Many towns adopted warships, whilst several purchased Spitfires and followed their progress throughout the war. In June 1944 the 4th Battalion held a large scale parade on Shalford Meadows in support of Guildford's Salute the Soldier week, members of the Battalion giving various weaponry demonstrations as well as showing off their capability as rescue and trailer pump teams.

However, the Home Guard also involved itself in matters nearer to home and undertook their own campaigns and raised money for other causes, some of them essential for the survival of the Home Guard itself.

In March 1942, members of the Lightwater Home Guard were shown Ministry of Information films and Will Hay comedies, a suitable charge being made in order that funds could be raised towards the cost of erecting a new headquarters for the Platoon. The event raised £5 towards the cost of the Platoon's new HQ, which the men intended to build themselves to save costs. A similar fund was also raised by Home Guard members in Chobham. A dance in West End, on Friday April 25th 1942, brought in the grand total of £31 16s, virtually covering the cost of a new hut for members of the New England Section.

Sgt R Adams of the Milford Platoon was the prime organiser of Home Guard social events in his village. Adams organised several dances and events which raised significant sums towards a number of causes. In July 1942, Adams promoted a dance in aid of the 'Bombs For Britain' appeal, raising raised £2 10s in this process. The local newspaper, the 'Surrey Advertiser' reported the event saying that 'as a result of this and a dance held recently at Milford Sgt Adams has sent £20 to the Ministry of Supply making a total of £100 forwarded to the Ministry by the Milford Platoon. £150 has also been raised for the Platoon Benevolent and Comforts Funds.' Adam's efforts also led to £10 being raised as a result of a dance held in the Chichester Hall, Witley, this time in aid of the Platoon's Rifle Club Fund. £23 10s was also raised for the 'Aid To Russia Fund', this being achieved as a result of another dance in August 1942, held in the local Church Institute, Mr W Smith's Band playing at both of the last two dances. By December 1942 the Platoon had raised £160 10s for various causes.

Many other Platoons raised funds for various causes during the war. In October 1942, for example the Windlesham Platoon sent £10 to the Queen's Royal Regiment War Welfare Committee to supply Christmas cigarettes to members of the Queen's who had become prisoners of war. Funds were also raised by the Thursley Platoon, to provide Christmas gifts of £1 for every Thursley man serving in the forces. A parcel was also sent to every Thursley POW. £28 raised by the Send HG Entertainments Committee during 1942, meanwhile, was sent to the Duke of Gloucester's Red Cross Fund for POWs. Perhaps the most successful Battalion at raising funds for POWs was the 53rd who, in early 1943, decided to support the East Surrey Regiment's fund in aid of prisoners of war. So successful were they at raising funds for this appeal that by December 1943 over £2,000 had been raised. Amongst the items funded by the 53rd Battalion were 600,000 cigarettes and 7,000 books, as well as parcels containing gloves, scarves and mittens that could be sent on to POWs. By the time the Home Guard had been stood down in December 1944, £3,120 15s 3d had been sent to the East Surrey Regiment's fund.

In December 1942 No.3 Platoon A Company 3rd Battalion raised £75 for their POW Fund at a dance and floor show. A competition was held, the prizes being 'a week for 2 in Prague after the war, a week for 2 at the Royal Hotel, Teignmouth, 6 Gallons of Shell, BP or Ethyl 48 hours after rationing ended (without coupon) and a pint of Best Bitter every Wednesday and Saturday for 6 months'. No record is held as to who won the prizes or when they were able to claim them!

Amongst the other events the Home Guard participated in were Summer Fetes, such as that held on the War Hospital Sports Ground, Oriental Road, Woking on September 16th 1944 . Many Platoons also gave Children's Parties. One such party was given by F Company, 6th Battalion in December 1943, 200 local children and evacuees being invited. Games were organised for the children who also received presents from Father Christmas.

## WEDDINGS AND FUNERALS

Weddings gave members the chance for very rare celebrations during somewhat trying wartime conditions. Platoons often turned out in strength to form arches of rifles and bayonets for the happy couple to walk under. The wedding of Sydney Allen and Brenda Watts in Puttenham in June 1942 seems to have also been a Home Guard social event! The bridegroom was a motorcycle dispatch rider with the local unit, whilst the bride's father and brother were also in the same Platoon.

Funerals were obviously somewhat more sober occasions but large numbers of local men always turned out to honour colleagues when one of them passed away. In May 1942, for example, 6 members of the Ash Platoon attended the funeral of local Home Guard J W Neville whilst the local newspaper reported Sgts Oxborough, Chuter, Stoner and Pte P D Maynard as being bearers at the funeral of Godalming Home Guard Bertram Earnest Jackman, a First World War veteran of the Queen's Royal Regiment. A large number of Woking Home Guards were also present at Brookwood Cemetery on the occasion of the funeral of Frank Stevens, who had died during a Home Guard exercise in January 1941.

Whilst all these events saw large numbers of Home Guards present, the largest turnout would come right at the end, for the stand down parades in December 1944.

*The band of the 56th Battalion at Horton Hospital, Epsom. (IWM)*

*King George VI meets members of the Virginia Water Home Guard. The King was the Home Guard's Commander in Chief. (David Carroll)*

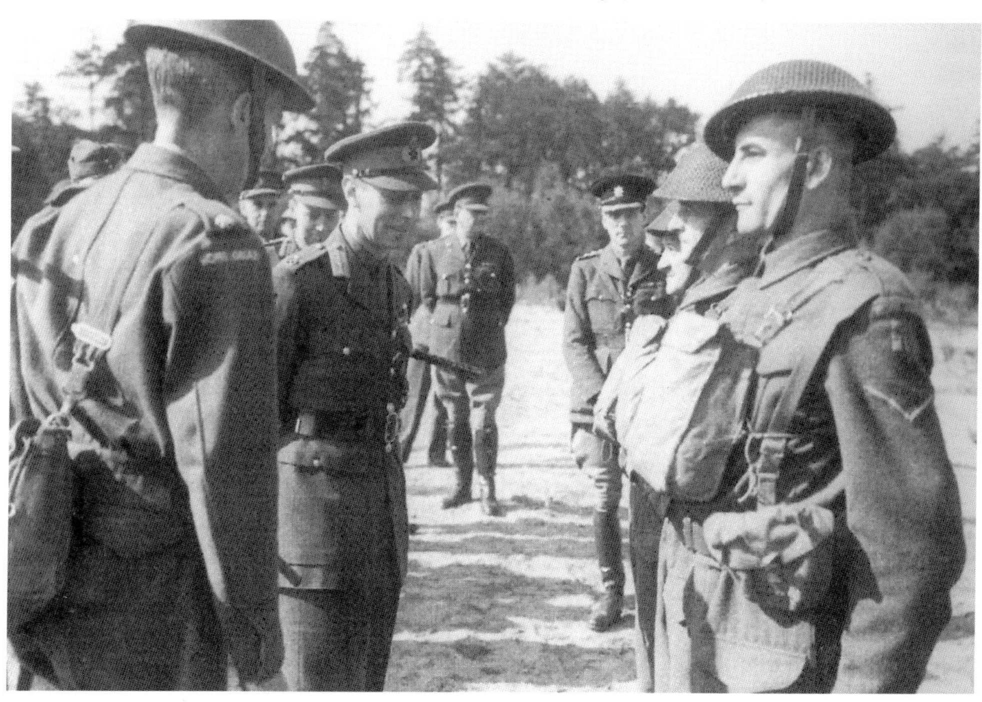

*Mr Vincent Massey, High Commissioner for Canada, meets members of the 51st Battalion's medical team having presented V Sector with a mobile field kitchen. (Mrs I Smith)*

*Christmas Card used by members of the 4th Battalion in 1944.*

# CHAPTER EIGHT -

# A VARIETY OF TASKS

## NODAL POINTS

By April 1941 the role of the Home Guard had begun to change. With relatively more up to date equipment and weaponry now reaching the Home Guard, units were now to be expected to play a larger part in the defence of their area. 'Nodal Points' were established across the country, the Home Guard being specifically detailed to defend these points and to hold them from the enemy until receiving assistance from regular troops in the area. The previous duties of observing and reporting were to run alongside this new role.

Whole towns were often designated as Nodal Points, although there were always specific points within each town that were particularly important to its defence. The 4th Battalion took over the main responsibility for the defence of Guildford in August 1941. The town was split into 5 areas, responsibility for its defence being divided up between the Battalion's A, B, C, D, and F Companies, E Company being held in reserve.

Cranleigh's defence was undertaken by E Company, 5th Battalion who now put several schemes into place to ensure the village's security. A series of road blocks was established, these being concentrated on the main routes into the village, which was surrounded by a boundary of barbed wire. One Platoon was to be used as a 'Mobile Column' the other platoons concentrating on static defence of the village. A 'Labour Corps' was formed, an appeal being made to local residents for assistance, as follows.

'The Military Authorities having decided that in the event of an Enemy Invasion, Cranleigh will become a 'Nodal Point' or defended village, a non-combatant 'Volunteer Labour Corps' is being formed to help the Home Guard. The work, which is listed and includes sandbag filling and camouflaging, will take approximately 24 hours. Men, particularly in the building trades, are wanted, but everybody is asked to help, putting his or her name on an attached form. Please sign now. Delay may be fatal.' A number of 'Home Guard Havens' were established to aid any casualties in the event of an enemy attack. Plans were also made to open local wells to cover any water shortages and youngsters 'enrolled' as messengers.

The 11th Battalion had responsibility for the defence of Woking. A series of measures were undertaken to protect the more vital buildings. Dennis Batten tells the story of the arrangements made in his unit. "The HQ building, the WESCo Power Station in Walton Road, was chosen to be the Platoon 'keep'. From there Lt Woods-Turner issued orders to all the battle sections which were deployed in surrounding buildings. I was stationed in the premises of Woking Glass, on the comer of North Road. Another section was defending a house at the top of Boardschool Road, the third section had its fortified base in a house on the corner of North Road and Walton Road. This in effect meant that every approach to the keep could be covered by one of the fire teams. If the Germans managed to overcome a single position its defenders could have retired to the keep under covering fire from the other sections." Detailed arrangements were also made for the defence of Old Woking, road blocks being established to ensure that no one passed without a fight. Pillboxes were also manned, many of these being well positioned to have a good view of all the surrounding area. The arrangements made were detailed in the War Book compiled by Lt B Collier of No.2 Platoon, B Company.

Anti-tank traps were reinforced, the 53rd Battalion continuing to man such traps on the approaches to Hampton Court Bridge.

The somewhat static nature of these duties did not satisfy large numbers of Home Guards. They still wanted the opportunity to fight. In June 1942, though, it was emphasised that there should be 'no withdrawal from Nodal Points whilst there are any men left to defend them' and that any attempt to train Home Guards as 'guerrillas' should be discouraged.

## MOBILE COLUMNS

In order to support the static defence of the Nodal Points, the majority of Battalions now raised Mobile Columns, comprised of men who would move to a particular area when it was perhaps under pressure from an invading force. These columns were often made up of younger, fitter men, perhaps those who had not yet been called up or who were in a reserved occupation. One such unit was formed within the 51st (Malden) Battalion during May 1941. Under the command of Major J R Carmel, the unit was comprised of volunteers from within the Battalion. Those who wished to join the unit had to be less than 45 years of age and willing to undergo a 12 week course of training.

A Mobile unit was also formed within A Company (Molesey), 53rd Battalion (Esher), members using bicycles which they provided themselves. It was not until 1943, though that a Mobile Column was formed in Cranleigh.

## STREET FIGHTING

Many Battalions raised 'Street Fighting' units, comprised of men specially trained in the arts of house clearance.

Two of Ted Molyneux's uncles served in the Home Guard, one in Westcott, the other in Newdigate. "One memory of the early days was of Sunday Platoon training in our road. Basically, it was for house to house street fighting. The Platoon would take cover in the gateways (supers fired blanks for effect) and, on the command 'Platoon will consolidate in the back gardens', would come in through the front door and out of the back door. Often we would be sitting at the table eating our Sunday lunch. Suddenly the door would be flung open and two or three men would come charging through!"

Ted Molyneux also remembers that "one of the Dorking Platoons was a crack one and often took part in operations to test defences. Sgt Bill Devon was the leader. Sgt Devon's daughter remembers her father's time in the Home Guard and recalls that "he was sent to an Army School in Birmingham to learn about street fighting, ie laying booby traps, attacking tanks, using toggle ropes to climb walls etc. After that he returned to Dorking and a street fighting group was formed. They dressed in denims, wore skull caps and plimsolls and carried toggle ropes and coshes as weapons. The group demonstrated the rights and wrongs of fighting in the street and were also asked to test the defences of Gatwick Airport and Nine Elms Gasworks in Battersea. In both cases they took the objective."

A Street Fighting Platoon was also formed in Woking and Dennis Batten can recall them demonstrating their tactics on a number of Sunday mornings between September 1943 and July 1944.

## MEDICAL

With invasion very much expected in the spring and summer of 1940, and perhaps for many months after that by those in the Home Guard, most Battalions formed first aid or medical sections to deal with the anticipated casualties. It took several months for these units to be formed, LDV/ Home Guard budgets not always being able to be stretched far enough to buy the necessary bandages etc. One of the first Medical Sections was raised by six members of the 51st Surrey (Malden) Battalion during the summer of 1941. Their numbers were increased somewhat when several local ladies asked to join the section. Although women were not officially allowed into the Home Guard until April 1943, the 51st Battalion arranged for the women to be trained to take an active part in first aid work should they ever be called upon.

All Battalions appointed Medical Officers, for example Major G H Hollis in the 4th Battalion and Major A R N Whitlow in the 53rd. Teams of stretcher bearers were raised and, as will be seen in a later section, members trained in rescue work and in how to assist civilian casualties. Stretcher bearer competitions were held and exercises often included tests on how medical units would deal with any injuries sustained during an attack.

## MOUNTED PATROLS

With many Battalions having a large and varied area to patrol, members undertook their duties using an assortment of 'transport' to get around. A wide variety of motor vehicles were used with many units converting or adapting cars or motorbikes owned by their members. Some Battalions, such as the 4th Surrey in Guildford, formed specialised transport sections to ensure that vehicular transportation was always available and properly maintained.

Some units, though found that motorised transport was not suitable for the terrain they had to cover and many favoured the horse as a means of getting about. Among the Battalions to use the horse were ones based on the Devon moors and the South Downs of Sussex. In all, some 900 horses were to be 'employed' by Britain's Home Guard, one such Mounted Patrol being established within the 59th Surrey (Addington) Battalion.

Harry Hart was a member of this unit. "In the spring of 1942 I was a little over 16 years of age and working in a factory in Purley Way, Croydon, making radio transmitters for the Royal Navy. A school friend who lived near me in Addiscombe told me that his father who served in a cavalry regiment in the 1914/18 war had joined a Mounted Home Guard Platoon in Selsdon. We decided that we would do likewise but would need to increase our ages by a few months. We presented ourselves to the Mounted Platoon H.Q. We were readily accepted and found we had committed ourselves to one evening parade per week plus Sunday morning and two all night guard duties per month.

"The parades took place in the Platoon H.Q., the Selsdon Recreation Ground or the playground of the Selsdon Primary School. The Platoon was commanded by a Lieutenant assisted by a 2nd Lieutenant and some N.C.O.'s . The Selsdon units had two observation posts ready for manning if the need arose, one was a room on the top floor of the Selsdon Park Hotel overlooking the golf course and the area to the south and the other located in a grain silo on the Addington hills above Featherbead Lane.

"The over night guard duties varied according to the locality. In some areas in addition to the provision of sentries at Home Guard H.Q.'s sentries would be on duty at vulnerable points i.e. Gas Works, Railway Yards, Bridges etc. The Selsdon Mounted Platoon did not take part in this type of guard duty but provided a three man mounted patrol of the Selsdon and Chelsham areas. These patrols started at 5pm at the Selsdon Park Riding Stables where the first task was to saddle the three horses. Our uniforms differed only from the normal in that we wore riding breeches and puttees and carried revolvers. The patrols went by various routes to stables at Chelsham Common.

"The horses would be fed and watered and we would get a few hours sleep before arising at 4.30 a.m. to muck-out the stables, saddle up and patrol back to Selsdon, usually by the most direct route. After stabling the horses we dismissed at 6.0am and I would then catch the first bus from Selsdon to Addiscombe to breakfast before cycling to Purley Way to start work at 7.30a.m.

"The summer patrols were very enjoyable with a possible stop at the Harrow Pub on Farleigh Common, which then was a typical country pub. I invariably had the job of standing outside to mind the horses. Legally I was still too young to drink beer and at that time I didn't like it so I wasn't too bothered. The winter patrols were another matter, moonlit nights were not too bad but with the blackout regulations some patrols were carried out in pitch black conditions. I put my trust in the horse and hoped he could see better than me. The other hazard was the icy roads, I hated the very steep hill from the stables to the Bird Sanctuary. It was fortunate that there were few motor vehicles on our routes as we didn't carry lights and car head lights were heavily masked.

"During the spring of 1943, in addition to the mounted patrols, I had to guard a Bolton Paul Defiant aircraft that was sited in Selsdon High Street where the garage now stands next to the supermarket. It was there as part of the Selsdon 'Wings For Victory Week' to encourage the sale of National Savings Certificates. As it was a mild night I and two other sentries had no problem in taking it in turn to sleep under the wings of the aircraft."

Amongst the other Mounted Patrols was the one formed by men of E Company 5th Surrey (Cranleigh) Battalion under the command of Sgt J D Marks JP. This section was administered by No.48 (HQ) Platoon and was responsible for patrolling parts of Pitch Hill, working in conjunction with the Cranleigh School Mobile Platoon.

Allowances were paid to those members operating such Mounted Patrols, the extra cost of running the units being duly acknowledged by the War Office. It was not until November 1943 that it was decided to reduce the numbers of Mounted Patrols run by the Home Guard , although even at that time there were still over 700 horses still 'in service' across Britain.

## SIGNALLING AND COMMUNICATION

The LDV's original duties of watching and observing meant that they always had to ensure that they were in close contact with other local military authorities and/or the local branches of Civil Defence. Any enemy infiltration had to immediately reported and it was vital that this information be passed on as soon as practically possible. In the early days, the pushbike was the main means of getting about quickly and members had to ensure that any in use were always properly maintained.

It was not long though before the motorbike began to be widely used. Ben Carruthers was one of those chosen to join a new Motor Cycle Section in Wimbledon. "I was recruited into the Home Guard via a request for motorcyclists to act as guides for our defence forces travelling southwards through south-western areas of London and into Surrey. I became a member of a motor cycle section in Wimbledon whose duties were designated as Signals and Reconnaissance. Its headquarters was the Wimbledon Drill Hall and we were housed in a building opposite St Georges Road, which had a workshop and garage behind it." George Brine was also a member of the 54th Surrey (Wimbledon) Battalion. "There were a lot of motorcyclists in the 54th" he remembers "and so at the instigation of Lt Norman Campbell a Motorcycle Section was formed. A Dispatch Rider Letter Service was run by the Section by which messages from HQ could be taken to each Company Office as well as the local police stations and County Hall, Kingston. Two riders were stationed each night at Wimbledon Police Station which had radio/receiver transmitter communication to County Hall. As the war progressed the number of motorcyclists began to reduce due some of the younger members being called up for military service so it was decided that we should train our own riders. Members of any age were now taught how to ride and perform the required duties."

All Battalions operated Motor Cycle Dispatch Riders, the 51st Battalion having at least one rider on duty each day at Battalion HQ.

It was not only vehicular methods of communicating that were utilised by the Home Guard. Pigeons were also a favourite, many members probably having their own coops of racing and homing birds. One bird, though, was to embarrass members of the 62nd Surrey (Norbury) Battalion when, during a demonstration staged for Lt General Brownrigg, the Assistant Zone Commander, the pigeon returned home instead of delivering its message to Battalion HQ.

By this time it had been decided that it would perhaps be better if the Home Guard relied on more than the bicycle and carrier pigeon to carry messages to and from other units. One of the GPO Battalions' duties became to form specialised Signals Schools, one such centre being established in Guildford. The Southern Railway trained their own men in signalling at their school in Gomshall. Several Home Guards who attended these schools went on to pass their newly acquired expertise to their colleagues. The historian of the 51st Battalion, for example, recorded that, in August 1943, Lt G W Alexander became the first member of the Battalion to qualify as a wireless instructor.

Elaborate plans were now formulated to enable contact to be maintained between Home Guard Battalions and regular forces, as well the various arms of local Civil Defence bodies. Telephone lines were laid and field wireless sets used by members to ensure that messages could be relayed far quicker than ever before. In July 1941 the 55th (Sutton and Cheam) Battalion acquired some newly requisitioned premises as its headquarters and immediately installed new telephone lines, including a direct line to the local ARP Control Centre.

Harry Hart also found himself involved in signalling. "After a year or so I was asked to join the Selsdon Signal Section to become the Mounted Platoon Signaller. I then spent many interesting evenings and Sundays installing telephone cable around the Selsdon area. The longest run was from the Platoon H.Q. to the Company H.Q. at Addington Palace. The route for our overhead cable was mostly across country. The last two houses in Selsdon were just past the pylon opposite the footpath leading to Selsdon Vale. I believe they are still there. From there it was across Odds until we got to Gravel Hill which we crossed using suitable trees.

By this time we were getting infantry radio equipment and I was getting more interested in army signals. In addition I was finding it difficult travelling to and from Selsdon because of my long working day. I therefore requested a transfer to the A Company Signal Section based in a house opposite Shirley Park Golf Club in Addiscombe Road. During this period I attended parades in the

Shirley Park Hotel whilst my over night duties involved operating the telephone switchboard for the H.Q. at Addington Palace."

Plans and/or maps were made available to unit headquarters to make sure that all commanders knew how best to pass on any information they thought necessary to make available to other posts.

One of the best surviving Battalion plans is the one drawn up by Lt J H A Whitehouse of the 10th Surrey (Chertsey and Egham) Battalion in April 1943. Lt Whitehouse drew up a map of the 10th Surrey's area, on which he showed the locations of all the Battalion's Company and Platoon Headquarters. Also shown were the locations of neighbouring Home Guard Battalion HQs, such as those of the 1st Middlesex (Staines) and 31st Middlesex (Upper Thames Patrol) Battalions, together with those of the NFS (National Fire Service), AFS (Auxiliary Fire Service), the ARP, Police and Observer Corps. Lt Whitehouse then showed details of the various telephone lines etc available at each post. These were either existing or proposed field lines set up by the Home Guard or circuits used by the ARP or NFS. The one exception to this was that the Battalion, having surveyed the area around St Annes Hill, a local high-point, decided that visual signalling methods could be used from this point.

In 1944 the two-way radio was introduced into Home Guard service. Peter Brook was an Army Cadet at that time and here remembers his brief period of contact with members of the Woking Battalion. "Two of us, myself (then a Cadet Sergeant) and a Corporal called Gordon Anscombe, were asked to volunteer to help introduce wireless into the Signals Unit of the Battalion Headquarters of the local Home Guard.

"I was already a short wave radio enthusiast so it was right up my street! The Armoured Corps was based at Sandhurst Military College and they were given the task of training the twenty or so Home Guard (plus the two of us) in their spare time.

"The Home Guard on the course were from the various Woking companies and also some were from the battalion headquarters signal unit. Theory classes were held in one of the classrooms of Woking Grammar School for Boys during an evening in the week and covered signal procedures and the speaking and technical techniques for using army wireless equipment. This was supplemented a little later on by the practical operation of No. 18 sets around the grounds of Sandhurst on Sunday mornings. We were picked up by army truck in Woking and took a packed lunch with us to eat after the work was done - with real army tea supplied free. The 18 set was carried on the back of one person and was operated by a second person standing at the open set behind the person carrying the unit. There was a system of tuning all sets working together by a netting call from the master station and then tuning the sending and receiving frequencies together on each set.

"We took a written theory examination at which I came second in the class which caused consternation among the elderly members of the Home Guard. The Battalion headquarters was somewhere in the Hockering area in a house and we went there a few times after the course, but the equipment had not been delivered so we could not set up the communication system. The next time I went, the house was locked up and there was a notice that the Home Guard had stood down. We never got off the ground."

All Battalions appointed Signals Officers and many Home Guards were commended for their work in this area. Among those to receive praise after the war was L/Cpl F W Thropp of Cranleigh and Cpl F H Smith of D Company, 59th Surrey (Addington) Battalion.

## HOME GUARD ANTI-AIRCRAFT BATTERIES

In the autumn of 1941 the War Office decided to transfer up to 50,000 regular troops from their duties on the home-based anti-aircraft sites to combat duties overseas. Although it was then considered that Britain was less at risk from aerial attack than it had been in previous months, General Sir Frederick Pile, GOC Anti-Aircraft Command, was still keen to see his sites fully manned and did not want any diminution in the numbers of those employed on ack-ack duty. He therefore suggested to Winston Churchill that Home Guards be transferred to anti-aircraft sites in order that the proposed transfer of men overseas could be carried through without weakening his command.

The first Home Guards transferred to Anti-Aircraft Batteries took up their duties in the Spring of 1942. The men now transferred were often volunteers, although with conscription having been introduced in the early part of the year, several of those 'directed' to the Home Guard were sent straight to the Batteries. This was sometimes a problem for those in charge of the anti-aircraft sites.

In his book 'Ack Ack' General Pile wrote that his commanders had to get used to conscripted Home Guards sometimes not turning up for duty, their enthusiasm for the force not always being as it should. Those that did turn up had to be pretty fit, and General Pile thought that this was not always the case with the conscripted men.

Isla Franks remembers members of the 59th Battalion being keen to get to grips with the enemy. "The order came from Battalion to select a certain number of men from each Platoon and submit their names. This was easier said than done, for they all wanted to be selected and the Platoon Commanders in the end had to take names from a hat. Once they had confirmed the selection, they had to attend special training and were entitled to wear a special flash. I put the flashes in envelopes to be collected by the Platoon Commandeers, but the men all managed to call in to HQ during the day to be able to have them sewn on as soon as possible. It was at the height of the bombing, and they marched to the Battery in Lloyds Park. The siren sounded, we could hear the drone of the planes and see the searchlights criss-crossing the night sky, and then the guns opened up. I was very happy for our men for I knew how much they were enjoying themselves and how enthusiastic and fired up they were. The trouble was they were just too enthusiastic and fired all night, practically non-stop, so that everyone had very little sleep, and the next day complaints came rolling in. On subsequent occasions they and to be more restrained, but they all loved it."

The 101st Surrey Home Guard Rocket Battery (originally known as the 108th County of London Home Guard Z Battery) was affiliated to the 61st Surrey (Norwood) Battalion. Members of this unit were responsible for the manning of 64 rocket projectors in the vicinity of Penge and Anerley .

When first formed in October 1942 the Battery had no operational equipment and had to construct its own site. The unit was always short of numbers and had to make regular calls on the Battalions 'attached' to it, including the 61st and 62nd Surrey Battalions, in order to build up its strength. Figures taken on November 1st 1944 show that the Battery was able to call on 48 Officers and 1,268 other ranks. This meant that members were only able to man 48 out of the 64 available projectors if each member 'worked' one night in eight, as previously agreed. In order to achieve full manning of the Batteries, however, it was decided to ask members to do one night in four instead.

The Battery's first Commanding Officer was Major G J C Welch, who held this position from October 1942 until March 31st 1944 when he was replaced by Major W A Cooke. Major Welch was then promoted to command of the 3rd Regiment with the rank of Lieutenant Colonel. He was awarded the OBE at the end of the war. The Battery lost 6 of its number killed in action during the war, a further six dying as a result of enemy action away from the Battery.

The 71st County of Surrey Heavy Ant-Aircraft Battery was responsible for manning guns at Norbury, Shirley, Mitcham and Raynes Park. These weapons were somewhat different to those manned by the 101st Ant-Aircraft Rocket Battery. The projectiles they fired were heavier than those used by the Rocket Batteries and were of either 4.5" or 3.7" calibre.

Those manning these guns had to be fitter and were, generally speaking, of a younger age than their colleagues on the Rocket Batteries. The training the men received was quite extensive and included 1 hours lecture and 1 hours gun drill three times a week from members of the Royal Artillery. Home Guards could also attend extra training sessions on Saturday afternoons. The guns were first manned on March 15th 1943 although it was not until April 17th that the Battery had their first taste of action. According to the units historian, "the following night sufficient men turned up to man twice the number of guns and many had to go home disappointed". The Battery was eventually to see action on 35 occasions. When the unit was stood down in December 1944 the strength of the Battery stood at 57 Officers and 1,225 other ranks.

Amongst the other Heavy Anti-Aircraft Batteries manned by Surrey Home Guards were ones based at Ottershaw, Kingston and Guildford.

More and more Home Guards were to find themselves being detailed to the Batteries as the war progressed. Altogether some 118,649 Home Guards were employed on anti-aircraft duties, the work they carried out being particularly valuable in the latter part of the war as the V1s and V2s began to be launched against the British Isles. The Home Guard, both those who had volunteered and those who were conscripted, did a valuable job. Writing after the war, General Pile expressed the opinion that without the Home Guard, Anti-Aircraft Command would not have achieved everything that it did achieve during the war.

## CIVIL DEFENCE LIAISON

The importance of maintaining good relationships with, for example, local air-raid wardens was recognised quite early and it was not unusual for Home Guards to be specifically trained so as to be able to help out the wardens when needed. Similarly, it was not unknown for Civil Defence members to form their own Home Guard units, although, strictly speaking, this was not really allowed.

The two bodies often co-operated for training purposes, In Malden, for example, members of the 51st Battalion had the use of the town's ARP Gas Chamber during April 1941 and October 1941.

Meetings were often held to co-ordinate efforts in the event of an air-raid. In November 1942, for example, local Civil Defence Commanders and Commanding Officers of the 51st (Malden) Battalion met with the Town Clerk at Battalion Headquarters to discuss their plans for the area.

Heavy and Light Rescue teams were formed by many Battalions. In June 1943, for example, members of the 4th (Guildford) Battalion were sent for training in Rescue Party and Trailer Pump duties. As a result, by September 1943, the Battalion was able to man two Rescue Party and Trailer teams each night. By the following November 14 such teams had been fully trained within the Battalion. In the spring of 1944 the 55th (Sutton and Cheam) Battalion were asked to find 200 men to undertake Light Rescue training

On June 12th 1944, the first VI 'flying bomb' was launched to be followed a few months later by the even more deadly V2. The Rescue Teams now had their work cut out but rose manfully to the task. In July 1944, the 51st Battalion's diarist recorded that they were fully co-operating with the Civil Defence authorities, noting that 'the name of the Home Guard has never stood higher in public acclaim than it does today".

By the time the war had finished 136 flying bombs had fallen in the 58th Battalion's area. A total of 142 fell on Croydon and one even fell on the Headquarters of A Company, 55th Battalion, killing one Home Guard and injuring 18 others. The work carried out by the Home Guard was praised by the Inspector General, Civil Defence, who was moved to write to the Home Guard's Director General to thank members for their 'magnificent help'.

***Woking Home Guards prepared for battle. These men are dressed for street fighting duties, wearing plimsolls and helmets specially camouflaged by sacking cloth, used to break up the outline of the helmet. Among the weapons on display here are two Sten Guns (front row, first left and back row, second left) and a Browning Automatic Rifle (extreme right). The rest of the Section are armed with Ross Rifles. (Andy Stevens)***

*Members of the Old Woking Platoon on a street fighting exercise. Note the member preparing to throw a grenade whilst the rest of the Platoon provide cover for him. (Andy Stevens)*

*Members of the 51st Battalion's medical section during an exercise. Note the SB (Stretcher Bearer) armbands. (Mrs I Smith)*

*Another picture of the 51st Battalion's medical section on exercise. The 'casualty' being treated here has had his leg put in a splint prepared through the use of a members rifle. (Mrs I Smith)*

*The James Walker Platoon's armoured car. This vehicle, constructed from an Armstrong Sidely chassis and layers of ¾ inch metal plates, made several appearances around Woking and even took part in exercises on Pyford Common. The unprotected wheels and tyres, however, would have rendered the vehicle almost useless in full scale military service. (Andy Stevens)*

*Signals section of the 60th Battalion in the grounds of Whitgift School, Croydon. Note the motorcycle despatch riders. Seated in the centre is the Battalion C/O, Lt Col Ward. (Reproduced by kind permission of the Croydon Advertiser Group)*

*Receiving and sending messages at a field signal station during an exercise at Tillingdown, Waldingham, May 12th 1942. (Reproduced by kind permission of the Croydon Advertiser Group)*

*Members of the Weybridge HG take a break during salvage work, February 23rd 1944. (Elmbridge Museum, Weybridge)*

# CHAPTER NINE -

# A PRIVATE CONCERN

With many factories and businesses concentrating solely on war work, their protection became of great importance to the country's continuance of the war. Roof spotters and fire watchers began to appear at many factories and several businesses employed staff purely to keep a watch on their premises. As soon as the formation of the LDV was announced, many employed in vital war work jumped at the chance to help out and hundreds enrolled in the new force.

Before long it had been decided by many concerns that it was better for them to form their own Platoons, linked to their local Battalion. Each unit undertook to solely protect their firm's property and at first rarely operated outside the bounds of their workplace. Volunteers often signed up on condition that they did nothing other than guard their place of employment. However, workers were allowed to join their local Platoon instead of the factory's unit. Some preferred to do just that. John Booker volunteered to join Chessington's LDV. "When the LDV was formed" he wrote "I was in the design office of Nash and Thompson Gun Turrets at Tolworth, Surbiton. This company immediately formed a platoon but I decided not to join since all the ranks above Volunteer were obviously taken by management staff and I did not want to work for the same people night and day." The platoon Mr Booker joined was based at Chessington Zoo, although the animals had been evacuated for the duration and thus their protection was not one of the Home Guard's duties.

Factory units were often combined for administrative purposes and formed into Home Guard companies, each Platoon maintaining its own individual identity. For example, No.16 Platoon V2 Battalion (later 51st (Malden) Battalion), which was then comprised of seven factory units, was made into a Company on July 30th 1940, becoming No.3 Company (Factories). In Guildford, G Company was made up of detachments from companies such as Dennis's, Vokes's and the Borough Electricity Department, as well as from the Borough Surveyor's Department, the local Technical College and the REME. No.3 Battalion (Weybridge) included D Company, comprised of 5 Platoons (Nos. 20 – 24) based at the Vickers Armstrong Aircraft factory at Brooklands and the 32nd Battalion (Croydon) was made up entirely of factory units within the town.

Some factory units moved between Battalions. In the early days the 53rd Battalion (V4 Battalion) had 19 factory units under its wing. When the Battalion was reorganised on April 29th 1942 several units were moved to other Battalions. These included the ones based at Cellon and Leyland Motors (to the 52nd Surrey Battalion), Kingston Gas Works (to the 52nd County of London Battalion) and Surbiton Water Works (to the 39th County of London (Metropolitan Water Board) Battalion).

Exercises were undertaken to test the security of the factory/business. One Battalion certainly had cause to fear the existence of a Fifth Column. On November 3rd 1940 a scrap of paper was handed in to the 51st Surrey (Malden) Battalion. An entry in the log book for the night reads that " a tracing was brought in yesterday by H E Cohen which had been picked up by an errand boy near the end of South Lane, East Malden. It represented a rough map of the factories about Shannon Corner on the by-pass and included factories such as Venness, Reid and Sigrits, Salmons and Peatlys – all doing important war work. The tracing was handed over to Detective Inspector Stutland, also my report to the (V Zone) Commanding Officer." The log book, unfortunately, does not record the outcome of this incident. There also seems to have been a bit of problem with security in Woking. The Commanding Officer of B Company 11th Battalion, Major J Farmer decided to check the security of one of the factories in his area. The Manager of the munitions factory at The Lion Works had told Major farmer that the factory was "absolutely impenetrable". According to his daughter, Major Farmer "dressed himself in railwayman's attire and proceeded to journey on foot from Byfleet Station, swinging railworker's tools and pretending to inspect the track". When he reached the Lion Works he "simply walked straight in unchallenged. Lack of security point proved!"

One such factory Platoon was established by employees working in the Experimental Design Office of Hawker Aircraft Ltd., designers of the Hurricane, Typhoon and the Tempest Aircraft. Its chief duty was originally the protection of secret drawings and documents stored in the firm's Design Office, located in the same building as the Platoon's own Headquarters.

Although Hawker's factory premises at Kingston did suffer at the hands of the Luftwaffe, the company's works at Brooklands, where the Hurricane was being produced, escaped largely unscathed. The same can not be said for the Vickers Armstrong factory, also at Brooklands, where large numbers of the Wellington bomber were being produced. Soon after midday on September 4th 1940, a squadron of Me110s attacked the factory, killing 84 and injuring more than 600. Many of the casualties were taken to hospital in armoured cars belonging to Home Guard units stationed at the airfield. This attack stopped production of the Wellington for several days, although parts for it continued to be made in other local premises, including a back room at the Woolworth's store in Weybridge. A further raid, on the night of September 5/6th caused damage to the ERA Company's sheds where the Hawker Home Guard Platoon had stored a lot of their equipment, including Ross Rifles and several tin hats, most of which were lost that night. Production of the Hurricane was halted for the day after two bombs hit the Hawker works, although at least one Home Guard did manage to fire off a few shots at the attacking ME110s with a Lewis Gun. The airfield was attacked again on September 21st 1940, although this time the damage was a lot less severe. However, one of the three bombs to fall on Hawker's factory that day failed to explode immediately and had to be removed to a safer place to avoid more serious damage. For his work in helping to move this bomb Section Leader Tilyard-Burrows of Vicker's Home Guard unit was awarded the George Medal, the first Home Guard to be so honoured. Volunteers W J Avery, C E Chaplin and E A Maslyn were also decorated for their bravery, being awarded the British Empire Medal.

Platoons were also established by several other aircraft companies, including Fairey Aviation in Addlestone.

Redwing Aircraft Ltd had been the original owners of the small airstrip at Gatwick, being based there between April 1932 and the end of 1933. By the time the war started they had moved to the Croydon area, having premises at Prospect Way, Croydon and Bensham Lane, Thornton Heath. During the war, the firm made parts for the Wellington, Lancaster, Fairey Battle and Boulton Paul Defiant and by May 1945 had returned some 1800 aircraft to military service. The firm's main operations were originally carried out in Croydon, but production had to be moved to Bensham Lane when the Croydon premises were damaged during the air raid of August 15th 1940. Still the firm suffered at the hands of the Luftwaffe, a V1 demolishing their Home Guard Headquarters, killing the NCO on duty. Altogether some 200 of Redwing's staff were to enrol in the firm's Home Guard, which was commanded by Major C H Cowham.

Several other factories in the Croydon area had Home Guard units based on their premises. 107 workers from S and R J Everett Ltd joined their firm's Home Guard, commanded by Lt S J Everett. 40 members passed through the Platoon based at J M Glauser and Son, commanded by Lt J M Glauser. One of the smallest platoons was that based at S M Stuart-Turner & Co. Ltd, which boasted only 18 members.

It was often impossible for Home Guard Commanding Officers to be able to get all their members together at any one time. Parades and training sessions were rarely attended by all the members and even rotas for guard duty had to be drawn up to take account of members employment commitments.

There were, of course, the inevitable problems that occur when arms and ammunition are given to those inexperienced in their use. A log book maintained by five Battalions in V Zone, notes an incident that occurred in the Surbiton area on August 18/29th. The report reads "accidental discharge of rifle in Factory unit of HG caused three casualties. Men now in hospital. One injured in both legs, one in the ankle and one in the thigh." The unit at Blackburn Ltd of Catteshall Works, Godalming also appears to have suffered some difficulties. The following entries appear in the firm's diary for 1941.

"March 19th (1). Another round was accidentally discharged by one of the Home Guard this morning at 5.5am. Position - Look above notice board in Guard room, top of wall and roof.

"March 19th (2) The Home Guard had a bit more firing practice this morning when another round was let off at 5.20am. Position - Second rafter on right of stove."

Some units were well placed to give other Home Guards the benefit of their expertise. Another factory unit to come under the command of the 53rd Battalion was the one based at Trianco Ltd. This factory played a special part in the manufacture of the Smith Gun, a weapon that was to be widely used by the Home Guard. F J Cummings was a member of the Trianco Home Guard Platoon and this is his account of the units work and of the development of the gun.

"The Smith Gun was the invention of Major W H Smith who was the Director of Trianco Ltd of Imber Court, East Molesey. It was designed as a three inch bore mortar gun for the defence of aerodromes if we were invaded.

"I was an apprentice to the man who made the first barrel out of sheet metal. At the beginning, all parts, including the shells, were made at the factory. The Home Guard unit was started by Major Smith. Although he never became part of it, he gave a lot of help and encouragement to the unit.

"When the gun was finally tested and into production three sets of crews were selected from the Home Guard to demonstrate the capability of the weapon. Number one crew pulled the gun and limber by van; number two crew consisted of two motor cycles, one to pull the gun and one for the limber; number three pulled theirs by hand. There were some fields at the rear of the factory, which was part of their property, where we were able to train and test the guns and give demonstrations. A small rail track was laid across the rear of the field, a trolley was fitted and to that was added the shape of a tank, made out of plywood. A wire was attached to the trolley, and this wire in turn went the full width of the field to a pulley, which was then attached to a car. When given a signal, the car would drive down the field pulling the trolley and we would try to hit the plywood tank (which I must say we became very successful at). There were also plywood models of aeroplanes scattered across the field which we had to destroy. After the demonstrations we used to instruct delegated personnel how to operate the gun.

"Home Guard units came to Imber Court from all over the country, including ones from the House of Commons. We also gave demonstrations to several RAF personnel.

"We had our own rifle range, which other Home Guards could use, and did most of our training at Imber Court. The Platoon guarded the factory and often combined with other units for parades and exercises."

As a result of this special relationship with the factory that made the Smith Gun, the 53rd Battalion was never short of the weapon. However, the guns eventually issued to the Battalion did not come from the Trianco works, being made at various Ordnance Factories.

Home Guard units were formed at a variety of factory and public utility installations. Several Gas and Electricity works across the county, for example, had their own Platoons. These included Platoons established at the Gas Works in Chertsey (No.22 Platoon D Company 10th Battalion) and at both the Gas and Electricity works in Kingston (53rd Battalion).

Dennis Batten worked at the WESCo in Woking. (The Platoon was) "originally formed as an LDV unit by staff of the Woking Electricity Supply Company (WESCo). Within a short time one or two friends of staff volunteered to join the unit, which eventually became a Platoon of the Home Guard. The number of members was greatly increased by the conscription of local men not in war service but in important civilian activities. This more than doubled the strength of the Platoon. Some of the original elderly members found they had to take a less active part and many of the youngest members were being called up for full time service. The Platoon was stationed with its HQ at the WESCo premises in Walton Road. The WESCo Social Hall on the third floor of the office block was used several evenings each week for the projection of training films etc., instruction on all types of weapon, Sand tray exercises, first aid and many other subjects. These were D Company events, so usually the attendance was good. Guard duties were undertaken every night from the formation of the LDV until September 1944."

Other units in Woking included ones at the GQ Parachute factory, Sorbo Rubber Works and at James Walker's, who produced their own armoured car. A further Platoon was established at Fairoaks Flying Field, where No.18 Elementary and Reserve Flying training School had been established in October 1937.

By 1942 Light Anti-aircraft sites began to be established at factories across the country, including, for example, one at Accumulators and Tabulators near Croydon Airport. A specialised anti-aircraft squad was formed to help protect the Vickers factory at Brooklands, coming under the command of the 3rd Surrey (Weybridge) Battalion. In Woking members of the Sorbo Rubber Works improvised their own piece of weaponry to take on the might of the Luftwaffe by attaching an array of Browning Machine Guns to a pram. A ratchet was added to this mobile anti-aircraft site, making it easy to adjust the guns to fire up at any angle. A more effective collection of anti-aircraft weaponry was established a few miles away at the Fairoaks Flying Field. Although not a front-line airfield, capture of this site by German Paratroops would have been quite significant. The airfield was therefore well protected by weaponry such as Bofors Guns and, at one point, quadruple mounted Vickers Machine Guns. These weapons were manned by the airfield's Home Guards as well as RAF personnel stationed at the field. Fairoaks also benefited from Heavy Anti-aircraft guns sited nearby and the work of this and other such units will be examined in a later chapter.

Bomb disposal became an important part of Home Guard work and by May 1943 the War Office had authorised the formation of dedicated Home Guard Bomb Disposal units with a maximum membership across the UK of 7,000. Several factory units had a part to play in this type of work. In Woking, Major Quilter of GQ Parachutes Ltd formed one such (highly successful) unit, leading to his being awarded the MBE for his wartime work at the end of the conflict. Men from GQ Parachutes would often travel up to London to help clear unexploded bombs dropped during the blitz. If possible, the men would salvage explosive from these UXBs and convert them into crude home-made grenades, another case of made in Germany, finished in Britain! A further bomb disposal unit was formed in Farnham at Crosby Doors Ltd under the command of the firm's owner, Basil Crosby.

First Aid Teams were also established. One such section was formed in Croydon, most members coming from amongst workers at Croydon Foundry and Standard Steel but also a few from Aeronautical and General Instruments (AGI) in Purley Way. The section was under the command of Sgt Jim Moat. The unit appears to have been very successful. In May 1944 a letter was sent to Major Smith, O/C F Company by Major C M Russell of 32nd Battalion congratulating the team on their efforts during a Sector Stretcher Bearing Competition, which they won.

It was not only factory workers that formed their own Home Guard detachments, the 10th Battalion included within its number two Platoons based at the local Veterinary Research Laboratories.

Office workers also joined up to protect their businesses, one such unit being formed in the village of Ewhurst. On August 29th 1939 Lloyds Bank relocated its Executor and Trustee Department from Threadneadle Street in the City of London to Ewhurst Place. A few months later, staff there formed No. 55 Platoon 5th Surrey (Bramley) Battalion to help protect the Bank's offices. This Platoon was one of those that benefited greatly from the services of many willing female helpers. The ladies formed a large percentage of the clerical staff employed by Lloyds Bank at that time, many of their male colleagues presumably having been called up at various times to the armed forces. The Platoon made great progress and, according to the Bank's booklet issued shortly after the end of the war, they "formed and developed such skill in strategy and handling arms that Ewhurst Place might have been expected to rival Stalingrad if invasion had come".

Platoons were also raised by male workers at various hospitals within the 56th (Epsom and Banstead) Battalion.

The principle of forming units purely to protect factories and local businesses was not a universally popular one. Joining a factory unit enabled workers to play a part in the protection of their workplace without having to also consider other parts of their locality. It also meant that members were not having to perform Home Guard duties elsewhere when those concerned should perhaps have been at work. However, most general service Battalions suffered from a lower than necessary number of members and could have done with the extra help of those who restricted their service to protecting their place of work.

By 1942 the operational role of the Home Guard was beginning to change and with it changed the role of the factory units. Factory Home Guards were now expected to widen their field of operations and play a larger part in the defence of their local community. In July 1941 the War Office had issued a leaflet entitled "The Role of the Factory Home Guard Units' in which it expressed the opinion that it was possible for Factory Home Guard Units to effect the best defence of their factory premises by co-operation with other units in their area.

The formation of Home Guard clubs after the war will be studied in a later section but among those worthy of mention is the 32nd/61st Surrey Home Guard Rifle and Pistol Club. Formed by ex-members of the 'factory Battalion' in Croydon and their colleagues from the Norwood Battalion, this club still meets every Saturday night in Plough Lane, Beddington.

***Members of the local Home Guard display some of their trophies outside the All England Club, Wimbledon. (All England Club Museum, Wimbledon)***

***Members of the Vickers factory unit. (Andy Stevens)***

*Members of the WESCo Home Guard. Dennis Batten is standing on the far right of the picture. (Andy Stevens)*

*Members of a first aid team in Croydon show off one of the trophies they won during 1944. (David Carroll)*

# CHAPTER TEN - THE SPECIALISTS

The previous chapter discussed the role of the factory units during the war and the work they carried out to protect their firm's property. Some larger concerns, though, decided it necessary to form their own Battalions. Although many of these Battalions had their administrative centre away from Surrey all of the following had at least a few Platoons based within the Surrey county boundary.

## THE 13TH SURREY ADMIRALTY SIGNALS ESTABLISHMENT (ASE) BATTALION

At the start of the war, the Admiralty's Signals Division was located in Portsmouth dockyard. The Division was broadly divided into two, the Signal School and the Experimental Department.

With the city often being a target of the Luftwaffe it was soon decided to move the Division to more peaceful locations. In August 1941, therefore, the Signals School was moved to East Meon (Hampshire) and the Experimental Department to Haslemere and Witley (Surrey). The Experimental Department HQ and wireless section was relocated to Lythe Hill House, the wireless production to Whitwell Hatch, in Haslemere. The radar section went to the King Edward School at Witley, the schoolboys being moved to an old workhouse at Hambledon. The Experimental Department was henceforth known as the Admiralty Signals Establishment.

Four hundred of the country's top scientists and technicians were based at Witley. Amongst their number was astronomer Sir Fred Hoyle and at least six Fellows of the Royal Society. A handful of naval personnel were also based at the school. It is arguably true to say that the Battle of the Atlantic was substantially won in Witley, as the benefits of their work on radar and its application to naval strategy and planning played a significant part in the ultimately successful convoy system and the war against the U Boat.

With all this hugely important work going on at the Establishment's various laboratories and offices in Hampshire and Surrey, the formation of a Home Guard Battalion was deemed to be highly necessary to avoid any risk of infiltration or sabotage.

Surviving records of the Home Guard set up by staff of the ASE are fairly limited but the Battalion does appear to have been relatively small. There were at least four companies within the Battalion, with Platoons at ASE detachments in places such as Waterlooville (Hampshire), Wormley, Witley and Haslemere, the Battalion Headquarters. When they were stood down in December 1944 there were only 21 Officers serving with the Battalion, including 6 Captains, 4 Lieutenants and 9 Second Lieutenants. The Battalion Commanding Officer at stand down was Lt Col P Alexander, his Second in Command being Major S J Moss.

Amongst the members to put in particularly dedicated service was RQMS F C Bruce of Wormley. A recommendation that RQMS Bruce should receive a Commander in Chief's Certificate for Good Service was made at the end of the war for his work in helping to equip members of the Battalion. Having enrolled in the LDV in May 1940, Bruce was originally a member of the 1st Buckinghamshire (Aylesbury) Battalion Home Guard, transferring to the ASE Battalion in March 1943. Certificates for Good Service were also awarded to Sgt F Phillips and Sgt H Hesketh. Others to be recommended included Sgt Longley of No.16 Platoon D Company, for his work in instructing other members in the use of the Northover Projector, and Sgt W Emery who constructed the Battalion's assault course and had a particular involvement in TEWTS (Tactical Exercises Without Troops) run by the Battalion.

The Experimental Department remained at Witley for a time after the war, becoming the Admiralty Signals and Radar Establishment in 1948.

## GAS AND ELECTRICITY

Soon after the LDV was first formed, the National Gas Council was requested to ask Gas companies in London to draw up a list of volunteers willing to guard their works against saboteurs. Similar requests were also made of workers employed in other public utility companies. A significant number of volunteers came forward from the various Gas companies and all four of the London based concerns formed their own individual LDV units. Their effort was rewarded on August 14th 1940 when the four former LDV Companies were finally recognised as fully fledged Home Guard battalions.

Once again surviving documentation is fairly limited but it would appear that at least two of these Battalions operated partly within the Surrey county border, although all four had their main sphere of operations in London.

The unit that was later to become the 52nd County of London Battalion was formed by members of the Wandsworth Gas Company, following meetings on the afternoon of May 24th 1940. This meeting was attended by the Battalion's original Commanding Officer, Mr L Baker and Mr A G Costelow, Personal Secretary to the company's General Manager and later Battalion Adjutant. With only 47 rifles at their disposal, use of the unit's weaponry had to be well thoughout. Those members who had used a rifle before were detailed to guard "vital points, including  large stretch of the Thames, against sabotage".

Those who joined Wandsworth Gas's LDV struggled to equip themselves in the early days. Even armbands were hard to come by. "Strips of blue khaki material were obtained and sent to the local printer, who stamped on each strip in bold type the letters LDV. These strips were then returned to us and volunteers from the lady members of the staff did the necessary sewing to make armbands." Premises to be used as guard-rooms, for training and as rest quarters were easier to come by, however, thanks to the assistance of the Gas Company. This even extended to the use of the Company's Sports Ground for training purposes.

When the LDV was first formed, in operational terms, the Wandsworth Gas Company's unit was very much a static one, concentrating purely on the protection of company property. They did manage to have contact with the enemy though as, on April 16th 1941, men from the Battalion played a part in capturing 2 German airmen who had escaped following the shooting down of their Junkers JU88 over Wimbledon. Several members of the Battalion also received praise for their work at this time in dealing with the results of enemy action, particularly Pte W Chance for his work in extinguishing an incendiary bomb.

Some gas company units were originally included within their local Battalion, for example the Platoon set up at Kingston Gas Works. This, though, was one of several Platoons transferred from the 53rd Surrey Battalion on April 29th 1942 when the Battalion was reorganised, being moved to the 52nd County of London Battalion. By this time Lt Col C L Sinclair had been appointed the Battalion's Commanding Officer, dating his appointment from February 1st 1942, the date that commissions were introduced to the Home Guard.

Of the other gas company Battalions in the capital, only that formed by members of the South Metropolitan Gas Company in Peckham, the 49th County of London Battalion, is likely to have had any involvement in Surrey.

Despite the Gas Light and Coke Company's Battalion being based in Westminster the company itself extended far outside the confines of the capital. Separate Platoons were established by the company at its various works throughout the South East, including No.34 Platoon (Gas Light and Coke Company, Staines, Middlesex) E Company 10th Surrey (Egham and Chertsey) Battalion.

Although three electricity companies also set up Home Guard Battalions in London, these operated within the confines of the city and its immediate outlying districts and had little or no contact with the people of Surrey. In areas of Surrey away from "greater London" many Battalions formed, or administered separate Platoons specifically designated to look after individual electricity company property, such as WESCo in Woking and the Borough Electricity Department in Guildford.

## THE 39TH COUNTY OF LONDON (METROPOLITAN WATER BOARD) BATTALION

The 39th County of London Battalion was formed in June 1940, its headquarters being based in Finsbury. The Battalion was commanded by Lt Col C D Shott MC.

Although recruitment was at first restricted to Metropolitan Water Board (MWB) employees, call ups to the regular forces meant that those employed in other industries were later recruited to the Battalion. The Battalion was responsible for guarding water pumping stations, reservoirs and Board property over a very wide area including parts of London, Middlesex and northern Surrey.

C Company's Headquarters were at Hampton, Middlesex but the Company included several Platoons based at the Board's Surrey installations. Amongst these was No.4 Platoon, based at Surbiton and commanded by Lt C G Sutcliffe. The Platoon's Second in Command was 2nd Lt H C F Moritz MM. Although at first linked to the 53rd Surrey Battalion the Platoon later became attached to the 52nd Surrey (Surbiton) Battalion

LAA troops were also on hand nearby though Battalion orders made it quite clear that No.4 Platoon was "solely responsible for the ground defence of the works; no guard will be sent by a military unit". If regular troops were sent in, however, the Platoon would take orders "from the regular Commander on the spot, whatever his rank".

No.4 Platoon was given strict instructions on how to deal with anything out of the ordinary that it might encounter. This included any attempt at unauthorised entry to the works, lights being shown, suspected signalling to the enemy, "indiscriminate talk" or "attempts on the part of civilians to obtain information". Any of the foregoing had to be reported to the Police and to the MWB Battalion's Headquarters, as well as No.16 Section Intelligence Corps.

Details were recorded by the Battalion of the location of local railway stations, post offices and police stations as well as telephone call boxes, river bridges, first aid posts, the ARP Report Centre, AFS Fire Station and bomb disposal teams. This included map references and their distance from Platoon Headquarters.

A training timetable was drawn up for each month. In July 1942, for example, Platoon training included the following sessions:
Monday 6th – Field training (19.30 – 21.30 hours)
Wednesday 8th – Weapon training, EY Rifle (19.30 – 21.30 hours)
Monday 20th – Musketry, bayonet and anti-gas training (19.30 – 21.30 hours)

The timetable for January 1944 included the following:-
Monday 9th – Weapon training (handling) 36m Grenade, EY Rifle, Northover Projector and Spigot Mortar.
Monday 23rd – Tactical weapon training and firing 36m Grenades, EY Rifles and Northover Projector.

Jim Ponsford was a member of No.11 Platoon, C Company, based at Walton on Thames. He joined the Platoon on June 18th 1940, having been deemed unfit for military service, rising to the rank of Sergeant in December 1943.

Paperwork retained by Mr Ponsford shows that his Platoon attended Bisley Range on December 28th 1941. A 'friendly' competition held between members of the Platoon resulted in Mr Ponsford gaining top marks, having achieved 4 'bulls' and 3 'outers' during the session. In March 1942 C Company were asked to supply 30 men to represent the Battalion at Bisley, a meeting that would also be attended by the Director General of the Home Guard, Lord Bridgeman.

Mr Ponsford still retains his training record card, an item issued to all members of the Battalion. The card shows that he reached a high standard of efficiency in all aspects of Home Guard work excepting signalling and first aid, roles usually only undertaken by a few selected members of each unit. The Company Commander, Major C J Alexander, signed each line of the card to indicate that the required standard of efficiency had been reached.

No aspect of Home Guard work was ignored. In July 1942, for example, Major Alexander wrote to the Platoons saying that "The Board's ARP Officer has kindly offered to arrange for a gas demonstration van and a qualified instructor to attend any of the Board's works for Home Guard instructional purposes. Full advantage should be taken of this offer." A further communication from Major Alexander concerned the raising of a commando section at the works.

No.11 Platoon held their farewell dinner on Wednesday October 18th 1944 at the Swan Hotel, Walton on Thames. Saying that the dinner was "the last legitimate excuse Home Guards could make for being away from home", Major Alexander told those attending that the Platoon "had gone a long way to enhance the good name of the Company". No.11 Platoon had started with 63 members and finished with 65. During its term, 120 men and women had passed through the Platoon, 24 leaving to join the regular forces, of which two, Messrs Curran and Wasley, had been killed on active service.

Jim Ponsford stayed with the No.11 Platoon until the Home Guard was stood down in December 1944. After the war he owned two fish shops in the area, becoming known to his customers as "Jim the Fish". He also became Social Secretary of the MWB Walton HG Social Club, a position he is proud to have held.

Among the other units established by water companies within Surrey was No.21 Platoon (East Surrey Water Company) D Company 8th Surrey (Reigate) Battalion.

## THE GPO HOME GUARD

The Post Office has a long tradition of military service dating back to the 1790s when the Controller of the penny Post prepared to form a unit to help ward off Napoleon Bonaparte's France. Since that time Post Office staff have served both at home and abroad in various campaigns.

When the LDV was raised in May 1940 GPO volunteers had rushed to enrol with their local general service company. Such was the fervour to enlist in the force that 50,000 Post Office staff had offered their services within the first few days, with training beginning almost immediately. By June 15th one of the local newspapers was publishing the week's training session for the Farnham GPO volunteers, which ran as follows:

Monday (8pm to 9pm) Drill
Tuesday (7pm to 9pm) Miniature Rifle Range
Wednesday (8pm to 9pm) Musketry (new recruits only)
Thursday (8pm to 9pm) Musketry

However, with priority being given to protecting GPO installations, it was soon decided that the best course of action was to form separate Post office units. The LDV was renamed the Home Guard at about the same time and in July 1940 the first GPO Home Guard companies (as they were then known) started to appear.

The GPO's Home Guard was split into 10 regions, each containing a number of localised Battalions. Eventually there were to be 40 GPO Battalions

Despite the fact that there was never to be a Surrey GPO Battalion the Post Office was well looked after by the Home Guard. Local units, such as No.1 Platoon (Egham Post Office) A Company 10th Surrey (Egham and Chertsey) Battalion and No.20 Platoon (Kingswood Telephone Exchange) 8th Surrey (Reigate) Battalion, played their part in protecting GPO property, however the main work in caring for the county's Post Office installations was undertaken by the following Battalions:

11th Sussex (39th GPO) Battalion
29th City of London (8th GPO) Battalion

Mr K Bell's father was a postman in the Croydon area before the war and worked for the GPO until 1947. When the LDV was formed he was working in the East Croydon Sorting Office and joined the unit that was eventually to become part of the 29th City of London (8th GPO) Battalion Home Guard. This Battalion was based at Southwark and covered SE and SW London District Offices and Battersea as well as Croydon. The Battalion was commanded at various time by Lt Col E W Young MM, Lt Col E R Shelley MM and finally Lt Col N W J Grant MM. The unit had struggled in its early days. Isla Franks's father was also a member of this Battalion and remembers the difficulties they had in obtaining the right uniform and equipment. "First they were issued with armbands, then forage caps and gradually the rest of the uniform until they really felt like real soldiers again, for the majority of members had served in the Great War. To start with they were issued with pikes and, to assist with their drilling, an enterprising carpenter member made weighted wooden replica rifles to give some semblance of order and rhythm."

The 11th Sussex (39th GPO) Battalion also contained companies that looked after Surrey GPO installations. The Battalion had its headquarters in Brighton and was comprised of seven companies (A to G) covering offices in Sussex, Hampshire and Surrey. B Company had its headquarters in Guildford and was made up of four Platoons, numbers 1, 2 and 4 based in Guildford and number 3 in Dorking. G Company's headquarters were in Aldershot, Hampshire. This Company was made up of five Platoons as follows, No.1 (Aldershot), No.2 (Farnham), No.3 (Basingstoke), No.4 (Woking) and No.5 (Haslemere). The Platoon Commander in Woking was Lt Spooner. A former RSM with the Queen's 2nd Foot Regiment, Spooner was, according to the Woking Review " a happy choice .. for his knowledge of small arms and grenades were unsurpassed." Lt Spooner was a postman by trade and when compulsory service was introduced into the Home Guard in February 1942 he found himself in charge of GPO Inspectors and Overseers, men normally his senior during the working day. So successful a job did Lt Spooner make of his command that a concert in his honour was held by members of the Woking Platoon at the Albion Hotel in the spring of 1945.

The duties of the GPO Home Guard units differed some what from those of the General Service units and can be summarised as follows:-

1. To provide guards and patrols at key points such as telephone exchanges and large post offices.
2. The setting up of a signals systems within the Home Guard generally.

This included:-

i) The training of specialist signals units to a standard sufficient to enable them to be able to act under operational conditions
ii) Advice to and collaboration with local units to enable operational signals systems to be established within the Battalion area
iii) The provision of Signals Liaison Officers to maintain contact with local Home Guard units and to assist with training and organisation of Signals sections within General Service Battalions
iv) The establishment of a Signals Training School

3.The protection of Post Office workers engaged in the provision and maintenance of telecommunications services generally.

A Signals School was set up in Brighton by the 11th Sussex Battalion and there was also one in Guildford. The School was opened to members of the press on Sunday May 31st 1943, a Surrey Advertiser reporter being one of those invited to attend. Opened in November 1942 the School was run by Lt (later Captain) Tomlin and served eight Surrey Home Guard battalions. The School ran a course every six weeks or so and gave Home Guards training on all aspects of communication, including morse code, switchboard operation, wireless telegraphy, the duties of dispatch riders, map reading and phonogram procedure and the phonetic alphabet. The reporter was evidently impressed with what he saw. "Reporters witnessed an interesting and efficient scene at a garrison signals office, where instruction was being given in signals office procedure under the command of Lt P Long. A typical message was broadcast to eight stations within 1 minute 15 seconds. Considering the time taken to train an infantry signaller in the Regular Army" he wrote "it is remarkable that many Home Guards, whose service is part time, have reached an equivalent standard in little more than a year".

In common with most other units, B Company 11th Sussex (39th GPO) Battalion held their final parade on December 3rd 1944. Meeting at their headquarters at the New Telephone Exchange,

Leapale Road, Guildford the Company marched behind the Deputy Company Commander, Capt A W Rice MM, to Stoke Park Mansion where the salute was taken by the Mayor of Guildford, Mr Wykeham Price and Major S D Pendry, the Company Commander. Also in attendance was the former Company Commander Major G W Beaumont. The parade heard Mr Wykeham Price pay tribute to the Post Office Home Guard saying that "upon them fell the vitally important task of maintaining communications, without which none of the Armed Forces could survive. It was a great responsibility".

B Company then returned to their headquarters in Leapale Road where the final order, "parade dismiss", was given.

## THE LPTB HOME GUARD BATTALIONS

The London Passenger Transport Board (LPTB or "the Board") was established in 1933. It owned, and was responsible for the day to day running of, the capital's transport system, including its bus, trolleybus, tram and underground services. The Board's area spread well outside the confines of the city, extending to place such as East Grinstead, Dorking, Reigate, Chertsey and Guildford.

When the LDV was formed in May 1940 the Dunkirk evacuation and the blitz were both still to come and nobody then knew quite how hard the war would hit the capital and its transport system. The Board had a lot to protect. Their area covered some 2,000 square miles, there were 82 bus garages and 31 tram and trolleybus depots, 181 railway stations, three generating stations and five overhaul works to look after, not forgetting all the road vehicles and railway rolling stock to care for.

When the LPTB's units were first raised they were formed into six battalions, each specialising in a particular aspect of the Board's work, including No.1 Battalion (Railways and Civil Engineer's Department), No.4 Battalion (Busmen South of the Thames) and No.5 Battalion (Southern Trams and Trolleybuses).No.4 Battalion had 31 bus garages to take care of, its A Company being based in Reigate. No.1 Battalion would have looked after underground stations and depots at, for example, Wimbledon and Morden and No.5 the tram and trolleybus systems in towns such as Croydon, Wimbledon and Kingston. The other Battalions would have mainly operated outside the county of Surrey.

In November 1941 the LPTB's Home Guard was reorganised as it was now thought better to organise the Battalions into localised units, rather than have each one of them looking after a particular type of transport. Six LPTB Battalions were formed, these now becoming known as the 41st, 42nd, 43rd, 44th, 45th and 46th County of London (LPTB) Battalions. The original No.2 Battalion was now designated to take over control of the Board's Surrey concerns and was now to be known as the 42nd County of London (LPTB) Battalion. Its Headquarters were in East Sheen and the Battalion was made up of 5 Companies and 21 Platoons as follows:- A Company (Mortlake Garage, Chelverton Road, Putney Bridge, Wandworths Depot and Battersea Garage), B Company (Norwood Garage, Norwood Depot, Streatham Garage, Streatham Depot), C Company (Croydon Garage, Thornton Heath Depot, Sutton Depot and Sutton Garage) D Company (Merton Garage, Morden Depot, Morden Station and Kingston Garage), E Company (Chelsham Garage, Godstone Garage, Reigate Garage and East Grinstead).

The 45th County of London (LPTB) Battalion was made up of 4 Companies and had its headquarters at Isleworth. The Battalion's D Company included 6 Platoons, 4 of them based in Surrey, ie No.15 (Addlestone Country Buses), No.16 (Leatherhead Country Buses), No.17 (Dorking Country Buses) and No.18 (Guildford Country Buses).

The Board's Home Guards formed mobile columns, machine gun and commando units and earned many gallantry awards over the course of the war, including that of an O.B.E. to 2nd Lieutenant W. B.G. Edwards for saving the life of a member of the 17th Sussex (East Grinstead) Battalion whilst on attachment to that unit. One Company even had the honour of mounting guard at Buckingham Palace on May 14th, 15th and 16th 1941.

In all, the LPTB's Home Guard built or converted 137 guardrooms and manned 76 strong-points during its 4 ½ year term of service and played a large part in keeping the capital's transport system going so smoothly and efficiently during the war.

## THE SOUTHERN RAILWAY

The story of the Southern Railway's Home Guard began in June 1940, when the company's General Manager gave his formal approval for the formation of dedicated LDV units across his company's region. Meetings were held at the Deepdene Hotel, near Dorking, on June 2nd to discuss formation of the Southern's LDV, Company headquarters having been transferred there from Waterloo as a precaution against air raid damage. Lt Col G L Hall (Assistant Engineer, Signals and Traffic) was appointed Chairman of a committee to organise the company's efforts, LDV Company leaders being appointed at the same meeting. Within two days 12,000 men had volunteered for service in the LDV across the Southern Railway, this number increasing to 18,000 within the first week. Altogether some 35,510 men and women were to enrol in the Southern's Home Guard between May 1940 and December 1944.

According to a contemporary list the company had "more than 35,000 steel bridges, 6000 plus brick arches and viaducts and over 2,000 route miles of track" to look after. Altogether some 841 points of varying importance were identified as being in need of some form of protection, including signalboxes, workshops, offices, depots and stations, in addition to the structures and permanent way mentioned above. The LDV was seen as having a hugely important role to play in ensuring the company kept going. One commentator summed up the aims of the company's LDV as being "to provide a trained body of its own men to give military protection to all points of importance in the railway, summer or winter, fair weather or foul, until victory is won."

The Southern were to eventually raise six Home Guard Battalions, the 28th Kent (1st Southern Railway), 25th Sussex (2nd Southern Railway), 12th Surrey (3rd Southern Railway), 21st Hampshire (4th Southern Railway), 22nd Devon (5th Southern Railway) and the 36th County of London (6th Southern Railway) Battalions. The Surrey Battalion was comprised of seven Companies, based in (A) Woking, (B) Feltham (Middlesex), (C) Twickenham (Middlesex), (D) Wimbledon, (E) Guildford, (F) Farnborough (Hampshire) and (G) Ashtead.

As can be seen, not all the Company headquarters were to be found in Surrey although some Platoons within the Middlesex and Hampshire companies were based within the Battalion's home county. Similarly, the Surrey sections of the Southern were not protected solely by the 3rd Battalion. The 2nd Battalion, although nominally a Sussex unit, included within its ranks four companies based in Surrey as follows:-

A Company (Redhill, Surrey) (Platoons 1, 1a, 2 and 3).
B Company (Deepdene Hotel, Surrey) (Platoons 4 - 6).
C Company (East Croydon, Surrey) (Platoons 7 - 10).
D Company (Redhill, Surrey) (Platoons 11 - 13).

C Company was eventually transferred to the 6th Battalion, becoming K Company of the London based Battalion. The Company had its headquarters at Selhurst and was responsible for suburban stations between Victoria and Croydon, as well as the locomotive shed at Norwood Junction.

Mr F J Wymer was appointed to lead the Southern's Home Guard, staying in that position until January 1944 when he retired to be replaced by Col S H Isaac. The man chosen to lead the 3rd Battalion in May 1940 was Mr W S Weekes, although he was to be replaced by Lt Col K R Ellson in August 1943. Ellson was originally Defence Works Officer at Battalion Headquarters, Waterloo and formerly an assistant to the Southern's Traffic Manager. The Commander of the 2nd Battalion was Lt Col E W Sheppard, who unfortunately had to resign his command on March 31st 1941 due to ill health, the Battalion being taken over by Lt Col C T Brett.

Amongst those to serve in the Southern's Surrey Home Guard were Woking based Ronald Andrews (a porter), Harold Boyd (a Sub Inspector, Eng.) and Ernest Rainbow (a porter/signalman). Brothers Alfred and Kenneth Gaylard , both from the village then known as West Weybridge (now served by Byfleet and New Haw station), also enrolled as did their lodger, Frederick Byde, a porter from Byfleet. Another porter from Byfleet, Robert Trower, also enrolled. Born on August 8th 1920, Mr Trower commenced service with the Southern Railway on June 28th 1937 at Walton on Thames. His Home Guard enrolment form gives his date of entry into the force as June 11th 1940, being posted, like the other gentlemen above, to A Company of the 12th Surrey (3rd Southern Railway) Battalion. He was transferred to Sunbury as a Tablet Runner (Porter) on October 10th 1940 and eventually saw wartime Army service as one of the Desert Rats in Montgomery's 8th Army in North Africa, later taking part in the Salerno landings during September 1943.

Becky Brown worked for the Southern at Woking and here recalls how she helped out the Railway's LDV in its formative days. "I became involved as I was an employee of Southern Railway and my department had been evacuated to Brighton, a long daily journey from New Malden. I applied for a transfer to Woking, to where the London West offices had been evacuated. I was offered a post in the newly formed LDV, the Headquarters of which were in the Station Master's office. He soon wanted his office back so the Railway slung one of its camping coaches just outside the station for the LDV to use." With women not being officially allowed to be members of the LDV/Home Guard until April 1943, Mrs Brown was given a clerical role that had no official position within the new force. The work she carried out, however, survived until the very last days of the Home Guard. "My first job was to transfer names and details of all men enrolling to record books, which were kept up to date until the stand down in December 1944."

After a while new quarters were urgently needed by the Woking Company and Battalion HQ staff. "The camping coach began to deteriorate" remembers Becky Brown "and a large furniture store opposite Woking Station became vacant. We applied for it to be requisitioned and, after a visit by a Brigadier on a very wet afternoon when we had buckets collecting the rain, this was granted. The store became Battalion HQ, A Company office and uniform and equipment store, as well as providing space for exhibitions for 'Salute the Soldier' weeks."

The Southern Railway had been issuing its own magazine ever since the 'grouping' in 1923. The origins of the 'Southern Railway Magazine' can be traced back a lot further than that, however, as the magazine incorporated a journal called the 'South Western Gazette', first published in 1881. The magazine was available at a cost of 4d in 1940 (1½p in today's money) and covered virtually every aspect of the company's day-to-day life. The formation of the LDV put the publication under some pressure, though and it was soon decided that it would be a good idea to provide a separate journal dedicated solely to the new force.

In May 1940 the Southern began publication of a broad sheet newspaper called 'Southern On Guard' (renamed 'Southern Home Guard' in February 1944). Published every two months the newspaper was free to any employee interested in the LDV/Home Guard, whether a member of the force or not. 'Southern on Guard' carried a variety of articles giving readers news from all six Battalions. In the early days it made appeals for new volunteers as well as well as asking questions of those who had already enrolled, such as "can you judge distances – practice it as you go along the street", "are you familiar with the surrounding streets and countryside" and "do you know the quickest way to the nearest police station or military Headquarters". The paper also sent messages to Home Guards, for example "make sure you know exactly what your job is when on duty" and "get all the training you can, it keeps you fit". Battalion social events, such as dances, darts matches and sports events were regularly covered. One of the first events to be mentioned in the newspaper was a sports day held at Richmond on June 26th 1940 which featured wrestling and boxing competitions. The paper also gave coverage to a Ministry of Information film called 'Shunter Black's Day Off'. Released to cinemas in the summer of 1941, the film tells the fictional story of an air-raid on a Southern Marshalling Yard and the work of Black and his colleagues in helping to extinguish the resultant fires. The title role of Shunter Black was played by LDV Volunteer Shea of the 3rd Battalion's B Company, Volunteers Turvill and Frost also appearing in the film.

The first few issues of 'Southern on Guard' also gave readers details of those who had performed some act of note in the course of their duties in a regular column entitled "Southern Railway Home Guard in Action!". Several Surrey men appeared in the column, the first such members being Section Leader W E Stevens and volunteers Comber and Richardson of B Company, 2nd Battalion for "locating position of a crater caused by enemy bombs and taking immediate steps to safeguard trains proceeding towards the spot", this act being noted in the November 1940 issue. Other members to be mentioned in this column included volunteers J Stockwell, J Dandy and R Lockyer of Purley, "for volunteering to search the line at a time of intensive enemy action and subsequently clearing the track of debris, thereby allowing traffic to be restored after a period of standstill" (June 1941); volunteer A Meager of D Company 2nd Battalion "for taking prompt action to report the discovery of a broken rail and also assisting a search for a person injured as a result of enemy action" (August/ September 1941) and Platoon Commander R Lassister and volunteers A Izard, A Coleman, E F Bateup, W E Biddlecombe, D W Newport and C J Bryon of D Company, 2nd Battalion" for dealing efficiently with a truck of timber on fire" (June 1941).

The Southern Railway Battalions were quite lucky in that they had many unique facilities available to them to help in the training of their volunteers. Rifle ranges were established in railway yards at and in office premises. One such range was immediately put to good use by those enrolling in Woking. A similar facility was opened at Surbiton in July 1942, the range having been constructed through a joint effort by the town's railway and general service Home Guards. Shooting matches were held at all levels, an Inter-Battalion .22 rifle competition, for example, being held on May 16th 1942. The victors on this occasion were the 6th Battalion with 859 points, 80 in front of the 3rd Battalion who finished second. Several more local matches also took place. The April/May 1942 issue of 'Southern on Guard' included a report of one such match featuring a joint team of the Southern's Battalion HQ and Kingston units against 'an outside Home Guard', which the railway won by 754 points to 750.

The training given to the railway units covered all aspects of Home Guard work to try to ensure that members were capable of dealing with all eventualities. On April 9th 1942, for example, 60 members of B Company 3rd Battalion attended a lecture on aircraft recognition given by the local ATC. "We attended our regular drill nights" remembers one volunteer "to learn the theory and practice of handling weapons and other soldierly skills, combined with talks on such other things as self defence and protection against gas. I have an indelible memory of the choking effects of Phosgene and great sympathy for those who were unfortunate enough to have been gassed – especially my own boss".

A lot of the training was done at a local level, often by experienced, ex-army, Home Guards. The War Office's Travelling Wing also made occasional visits to the Battalions as it did the rounds of other units in the vicinity. The railway also had two unique facilities available for its members, one of these being the railway's travelling Cinema Coach. Constructed in 1939 to accommodate 56 people, the coach was originally intended to be used to show publicity films to interested members of the general public. The onset of war changed all that, however and the coach spent the next few years touring the Southern Railway showing ARP and Home Guard training films to members of the railway's staff. First used on July 24th 1940, the coach visited all six Battalions during the course of the war.

The other facility available to the Southern's part time army was the company's Home Guard training school at Gomshall, near Dorking. Situated close to Gomshall Station, the school gave members the chance to 'get away from it all' to the relatively peaceful surroundings of the Surrey countryside to train, hopefully, without any interruption. The school was loosely based on the one established at Osterley Park and offered attendees a full range of training activities. In mid-week the camp was used to train potential NCOs or junior officers. Those attending had to be in possession of a proficiency badge and had to have attended a minimum number of parades during a specified period. The course provided members with a pretty full week, a typical week's schedule including instruction on anti-tank rifles, grenades, camouflage and battle craft. An assault course was also available as was a miniature firing range, with Thursday afternoons being given over to shooting competitions. At weekends the school was available to Battalions on a rota basis, accommodating up to 120 men at a time, and volunteers were urged to approach their Platoon Commander to make arrangements to attend. Once again those attending the school found themselves with plenty to occupy their time, including potato peeling on the first afternoon. The school was very popular and gave members a very good grounding in Home Guard matters. It also provided an opportunity for those belonging to Battalions many miles away from each other to socialise and learn from each other's experiences, 5 Battalion and 46 Company Commanders, for example, attending a get together at the school on the weekend of July 10th/11th 1943.

The Battalions held many exercises to put new found skills to the test, 'fighting' alongside and against other railway units as well as local general service Battalions. The first such exercise held by the 2nd Battalion took place in Redhill on June 28th 1941 in conjunction with the 8th Surrey (Redhill) Battalion. The day started with a parade and inspection by Lt Col Sheppard, field operations being held from 6pm to 8pm. 800 men took part in the day's events. Writing after the war Lt Col Sheppard, commentating that it was the first time the Officers had commanded their units in the field, said that several mistakes had been made during the day but that 'useful lessons were learned by all'. The day was reported by 'Southern on Guard' under the heading 'Vigilance Leads To Victory!". The newspaper also carried a report of an exercise held in Wimbledon on May 7th 1941 when 47 members of the railway Platoon fought off an attacking force, only 15 of the aggressors still being 'alive' when darkness fell and the exercise ended. The defensive position manned by the Wimbledon men held firm throughout the exercise. A further exercise was held at Deepdene in 1941 when it was decided to test the defence of the railway's new headquarters. B Company of the 2nd Battalion manned the defence and once again "a number of useful lessons were learned". A spigot mortar exercise was held by the 3rd Battalion's A Company on Chobham Common on June 19th 1943, 16 teams competing against each other in a competition that included firing at a moving 'tank'.

All these events provided very useful information to unit commanders as to the state of readiness of their commands. Several mentions were made of these exercises in the columns of 'Southern on Guard', although the light hearted side of the Home Guard was not forgotten either. A cartoon in the August/September 1942 edition showed a commanding officer addressing his men saying "I trust you all benefited from your manoeuvres", not seeing the rabbits held behind the backs of his men!

All this training meant that the Southern Railway was able to boast six very efficient and capable Battalions. The regard the units were held in is evidenced in an entry in the April/May 1942 edition of 'Southern on Guard' under the heading 'Envy'. The article ran as follows. "Ash Crossing Gates. Ash members moving off from station. Platoon Officer approached by passing motorist who stated "that is a jolly fine section. I wish mine were half as good'."

The Southern trained 1,617 men in anti-aircraft defence work during the war and were able to mount 18 Anti-aircraft Troops at various locations across the region. Of these, 17 were Light Anti-aircraft (LAA) troops with one Heavy (HAA) Troop being in situ on the Isle of Wight. In Surrey, LAA Troops were posted at Guildford and Woking Stations. At Stand Down at the end of 1944, 22 Officers and 475 other ranks were still serving with the railway's Light Anti-aircraft Batteries.

The railway's Battalions often operated in extremely dangerous circumstances, with railway installations being an obvious target for the Luftwaffe. Many Southern Railway employees lost their lives during the war, among them Pte B R Dart of C Company 3rd Battalion who, according to 'Southern on Guard' "was the victim of enemy action whilst performing his normal railway duties" and Carshalton member Pte W Leach who died on duty on May 12th 1942.

The Southern's Battalions were stood down at the end of 1944 along with general service units throughout the country. The Surrey companies of the 2nd Battalion held their last parade in Redhill on November 25th along with the Battalion's E Company from Horsham. The farewell parade of the 3rd Battalion was held in Woking on Saturday 2nd December. The last issue of 'Southern Home Guard' appeared in January 1945, the front page carrying the message "Good Luck – and be proud of your Service".

## THE 34TH COUNTY OF LONDON (LONDON RIVER SOUTH) BATTALION AND THE 31ST MIDDLESEX BATTALION, UPPER THAMES PATROL.

Even before the formation of the LDV, several private boat owners had decided to form their own mobile defence units to help protect the River Thames, utilising their boats to patrol the non-tidal waters between London Bridge and Lechlade in Wiltshire. In May 1940 the UTP became the first Inland Water Patrol to be officially recognised within the newly formed LDV. (A one-page calendar prepared by the Patrol's Group HQ Staff in 1943 proudly reminds everyone that boats were supplied by Patrol members to help with the May 1940 evacuations from Dunkirk, this including the Motor Launches 'Bobel', 'Constant Nymph' and 'Surrey'.)

The task of guarding the river between London Bridge and Lechlade was eventually undertaken by three Home Guard units. The section from London Bridge to Teddington Lock was looked after by the 34th County of London (London River South) Battalion, whilst the area between Teddington and Lechlade was patrolled by the 31st Middlesex (Upper Thames Patrol) and the 12th Berkshire (Upper Thames Patrol) Battalions. These units undertook the protection of locks, weirs, bridges and pumping stations, although other local Platoons were also on hand to guard these and other important points along the riverbank.

For the UTP's purposes, the Thames was divided into 'stretches' of about 16 miles in length. A UTP command was established for each stretch, each having its own Patrol Commander. Existing documentation shows that in 1943 the overall UTP Commander was Col. Sir Ralph Glynn, Bart., MC, MP, the instigator of the Patrol. His deputy was Lt. Col. T N James CB, MVO. The 12th Berkshire Battalion was commanded by Lt. Col. L A E Price-Davies VC, CB, CMG, DSO and was comprised of individual patrols based in places such as Oxford, Sonning, Henley and Reading. The Middlesex Battalion, meanwhile, was commanded by Lt. Col. The Hon. T P P Butler DSO, and was comprised as follows:

Middlesex Flotilla (Teddington) c/o Major F N Griffin (Promoted Lt. Col. in August 1943 and given the position of Commander, 31st Middlesex Battalion), A Company (Kingston) c/o Major R H Turk, B Company (Sunbury, Middlesex) c/o Major T J Moore, C Company (Staines, Middlesex) c/o Major C F Bell CBE, DSO, OBE.

Members of the patrols at first wore navy-style uniforms although these were later 'swapped' for the outfits worn by the LDV/Home Guard. Members also wore special badges identifying themselves as members of the UTP

W F Peer was a member of the UTP in Kingston and these are his recollections of his time in the Battalion.

"I enlisted at the local Police Station on May 15th 1940" he remembers "and shortly afterwards was posted to Turks Albany Boathouse in Kingston, owned then by Richard Turk who eventually commanded the unit.

"I was a 28 year old married man with a young son when Anthony Eden's call came and had no previous military experience, so I had to learn on the job with a lot of help from old soldiers of the 1914-1918 war who were with us. Being then a rather shy and reserved young man one had to learn quickly and, as the stripes began to gather on my arm, so did the responsibilities that go with it. When in due course one was in charge of a patrol, lecturing or especially taking over at a Company parade inhibitions had to be subdued despite the sweat and fears. My professional work came under the "essential work order" so the war years were spent on my work and Home Guard duties. In my spare time I dug for victory and did a bit of fire watching at night.

"This Company of the 31st Middlesex Battalion consisted of four Platoons, two land based and two water-born. These latter two consisted mainly of sailing club members and had a separate headquarters. The Platoon I was a member of consisted of the most physically able people whose task was to patrol the Thames towpath from Teddington Lock to Hampton Court.

"My unit was on duty for one night a week from around 7.30pm to stand down at 6.30am the following day with no breaks during the night; a continuous patrol. This was found to be very tiring when one had to start work again at 8am. Later on our duty was revised to protect Teddington Lock and weir for a whole night with a base at the lock keepers hut within the lock area.

"Regular parades and exercises were on Sunday mornings with occasional lectures at HQ by PSIs (Permanent Staff Instructors), weapon training, tactics and explosives. On several occasions attendances were made at Bisley and Pirbright for live firing practice and grenades. At least once we had a training weekend with a regular army unit. Whole night exercises were also undertaken with our own Company's Platoons.

"On a lighter note, one incident occurred which I found amusing although the laugh was on me, so I recall it here. I persuaded a near neighbour to join our unit, but in uniform he appeared to be other than a credit to us. However, we pressed on and one evening went to Ham and Petersham for small arms firing. Full instruction was given by me as to the handling of the weapon and best position for shooting from the prone position. Having done this to my satisfaction I gave the order to fire the five rounds in the rifle. To my amazement he fired all five rounds in a few seconds so I was ready to tell him off, especially when I looked at the target 25 yards away with a one inch bulls-eye and could see no sign of a hit. This amazement was even more profound when pulling the target back it was seen that all five shots were over-lapping in the centre of the bull. You will have guessed by now that as he explained he was a sniper in the First World War. Unfortunately he must have been bored with us amateurs for he wouldn't take an instructors job with us and retired after a short time. A lesson was learned here; don't judge by appearances. The Home Guard was a very serious business and was often quite dangerous. Within out two land based Platoons one man was drowned in the lock and another killed on the firing point during grenade practice, with several others injured when a grenade exploded in the discharger cap at the end of a rifle."

Desmond Davidson enrolled in the Patrol in Shepperton, a town then in Middlesex but, following reorganisation of county boundaries, now officially part of Surrey. "About a month after my 18th birthday I went to Sunbury Police Station to join the LDV. In no time I was told that once or twice a week I was required to guard Shepperton Lock and I would be under the command of a Lt Hoole. I kept guard in company with two friends, Noel Dunthorne and Jack Marston. Jack was a great friend and was soon to join the Royal Navy. Tragically in 1941 he was lost at sea whilst serving as a gunner on an oil tanker. When on duty we liased with the flotilla section whose crews cruised between the locks. I particularly remember that we became very pally with the owner and crew of the Motor Cruiser 'Egret'." Battalion Part II orders dated January 16th 1942 show that, shortly after he joined the Royal Armoured Corps, Davidson was awarded a Certificate for Good Service for his work in the Home Guard. This award particularly relates to an incident on the night of November 29th 1940 when Davidson was injured whilst trying to deal with some incendiary bombs that had fallen on a local farm.

The 34th County of London (London River South) Battalion would have had slightly less involvement within Surrey, dealing as it did with the short part of the river within the county downstream from Teddington Lock.

Many boat owners had expressed their concern that the Thames might end up being looked on as a dividing line between county administrative areas, rather than as an area that itself needed looking after. The River Company LDV was formed in May 1940 as a response to these concerns. Eight motor launches, mainly manned by members of the Little Ship Club, were used to patrol the river below Teddington, the vessels being armed with two Ross Rifles in addition to any arms the owners carried themselves. Unfortunately a dispute with the Royal Navy led to the unit being disbanded in the autumn of 1940.

Members of this disbanded unit now offered their services to London District Command and eventually the 34th Battalion was formed under the command of Col E C Heath CVO DSO. A submission to Charles Graves's book, 'The Home Guard of Britain', recalls that the Battalion counted amongst its number "a KC, a goldsmith, two engineers, a Harley Street specialist, a physiotherapist, two solicitors and an editor". Amongst the others to join the river units was George Allison, Manager of Arsenal Football Club between 1934 and 1947. Mr. Allison, though, is likely to have been more involved with the London end of the Battalion area.

As well as river borne patrols, the Battalion also mounted Machine Gun posts at various points along the river. However, although its area extended between Teddington and London Bridge, the Battalion seems to have been mainly involved with the easternmost part of this stretch of the river.

***Jim Ponsford, 39th County of London (MWB) Battalion. (Jim Ponsford)***

*Southern Railway men parade at Redhill, a little over 1 year since the LDV was first formed. (Southern Railway)*

*Southern Railway men guard the entrance to Boxhill Tunnel, Dorking. (Southern Railway)*

*A Pillbox built and manned by men of the Southern Railway. Situated off Blackhorse Road, Woking this Pillbox would have served to protect an important bridge on the routes out of Woking, to towns such as Aldershot, Bournemouth, Basingstoke and Poole. (Paul Crook)*

*The Southern Railway's Cinema Coach. (Southern Railway)*

*Men of the Southern Railway's Home Guard on camouflage exercise at Gomshall. (Southern Railway)*

*A disused coach served as an indoor firing range at Gomshall camp and was available for night as well as day-time instruction and practice. (Southern Railway)*

# CHAPTER ELEVEN -

# A UNIFORM FORCE

## UNIFORM

As has already been seen, the issue of uniform to the LDV was not particularly quick, many volunteers choosing to use clothing and equipment they had retained from the First World War. Often civilian clothes were worn with just the LDV armband to show that the wearer was a member of Eden's volunteers. With many of these early volunteers also carrying various and assorted, often historic, weapons the general appearance of the LDV must have looked rather chaotic on occasions. "It was laughable really" remembers John Burrows, "parading on the common with just an LDV armband and a broomhandle and having to hand them in for the next men on duty."

The Government's promise of uniform was soon met, however, although the LDV/Home Guard were not particularly pleased with the quantity and quality of the first items they received. The first item of uniform to appear in any great number was the field service cap. These arrived in Guildford on July 6th, 1940. It is said that these caps were issued to units on a priority basis , before any other item was ready, in order that men wearing this "uniform" would not be thought of as terrorists by any invading German troops, although the German leadership had already said they would treat Home Guards as Franc-Tireurs (that is, members of "murder-bands") and that they would deal with them as such if any were captured.

The first battledress to appear in any quantity were the universally unpopular denim 'overalls'. These were issued to the Battalions during the summer of 1940, Guildford men receiving theirs at the same time as the field service caps. This 'uniform' was often rather ill fitting and was worn over the member's civilian clothing. It did nothing to improve the smartness of the men. By the end of June 1940 most volunteers in Limpsfield had been issued with denims as well as boots and leather gaiters. In Malden the Company stores had been started off with a 'stock of 3 caps (6 ¼"), 3 blouses and 4 pairs of trousers' on July 19th 1940. In Dorking, meanwhile, the 'Dorking Advertiser' reported that the LDV's parade of July 14th had seen all the men parade in uniform.

The speed at which steel helmets were issued to the volunteers also caused adverse comment among the men, not helped by the fact that they could be brought in high street shops. So serious a problem was this that an entry in the diary of the 55th Battalion states that Company Commanders there would no longer consider themselves responsible for the safety of their men during and after air raids if the helmets were not to be forthcoming. This problem began to resolve itself, however when helmets were issued to several units in the late summer of 1940.

Other items were also being received including greatcoats, gas masks, first aid packs, haversacks, eyeshields, box respirators and blankets.

At the end of July 1940 the name of the force was changed from the LDV to the Home Guard and "LDV" armbands were therefore withdrawn. These were replaced by khaki "Home Guard" armbands. By the middle of 1941, however, the Home Guard armbands had also been replaced, by "Home Guard", County (SY) and Battalion flashes.

In August 1940 the Battalions were affiliated to county regiments, the Surrey Battalions being affiliated to the Queen's Royal and East Surrey Regiments. Regimental cap badges were issued to be worn on member's field service caps.

With winter not far off, several local communities began to organise fund raising events to enable clothing such as woollen gloves and socks to be made or purchased for their Home Guards. Dances and social events were held in aid of Home Guard comforts, some units even tried to raise sufficient funds to enable them to build themselves new huts or headquarters. Boots and greatcoats were also now issued to all Battalions, their importance being recognised with the long cold nights of winter fast approaching.

By December 1940 the first issue of serge battledress had begun, promising a significant improvement in both smartness and comfort. Guildford men received theirs in March 1941 and the unpopular denims were 'returned to store'. The 55th Battalion had received 1,500 serge battledress uniforms and 1,400 greatcoats by November 17th 1940, a few months earlier than those in Guildford. Boots and greatcoats were also now issued to all Battalions, their importance being recognised with the long cold nights of winter fast approaching. March 1941 saw the first issue of service respirators to units such as the 51st Surrey (Malden) Battalion.

Some Platoons were perhaps able to look smarter than others. John Burrows remembers one of his colleagues in the Bagshot Platoon. "Sgt Robinson was, by trade, a presser and part time tailor. Whenever we had a parade they we would ask Sgt Robinson to press our uniforms for us. We were always very well turned out. Sgt Robinson's business was in the premises now used by Fellows Off Licence".

Other 'uniforms' had started to appear by the summer of 1942, June seeing the first issue of sniper suits to the Home Guard. Designed to camouflage men working in open country, these suits were often made by members of the WVS and were a highly effective way of blending in with the local scenery.

Among the other items that could be worn by Home Guards were Proficiency Badges, Long Service Chevrons and medal ribbons from previous campaigns.

By stand down in December 1944 the uniform received by the average Home Guard would have included the following items: battledress blouse, battledress trousers, greatcoat, boots, gum boots (occasionally), field service cap, cap badge, steel helmet and chin strap, anklets, leather waist belt, rifle, sling, haversack, eyeshields, field dressing, woollen gloves, HG shoulder title and distinguishing flashes, blanket, pouches, cape and camouflage net.

Ownership of the various items of uniform issued to Home Guards remained with the War Office and members were often asked to sign forms acknowledging the fact. On Stand Down, however, it was announced that men could keep any uniform still in their possession and it is not unknown for greatcoats to still be in use today.

## WEAPONS

Despite Eden's promise that the LDV would be armed, the promised weaponry did not arrive for several weeks and, in some cases, not for several months. Mention has already been made of the lengths gone to by some units to improve their armoury, stocking themselves up with weapons that should have been put to store many years before. Appeals were made in several areas for residents to loan privately owned shotguns and revolvers to the LDV. Ammunition was always in short supply in the early days, the 4th Battalion being moved to purchase 10,000 rounds of small arms ammunition (SAA) privately in August 1940. Improvisation was very much the order of the day, typified by the large amount of home-made Molotov Cocktails that found their way into LDV usage.

Over the next four years the Home Guard were to be issued with a wide variety of weapons, some more efficient than others.

Listed below is a selection of some of the more commonly issued weapons:

**Bayonets -** Issued in large numbers to the LDV/Home Guard, the 4th Battalion had a stock of over 1,000 bayonets by December 1941.

**Blacker Bombard (Spigot Mortar)** - A popular anti-tank weapon, first issued to the Home Guard in the autumn of 1941. Could fire either 12lb anti-personnel or 20lb anti-tank missiles. Its issue to the Home Guard seems to have been undertaken under a veil of secrecy. The Limpsfield historian recalled "a mysterious looking weapon, obviously pertaining to the genus artillery" arriving at their Thornhill Training Hut without members being given any real information about their new weapon.

**Boys Anti-Tank Rifle** - A large number of this rather outdated weapon were issued to the Home Guard during 1943. The Farnham Home Guard were issued with this weapon "but briefly", according to Ronald Hack who also expressed the opinion that it was more likely to harm the firer than its intended target!

**Bren Gun** - The Bren was badly needed by regular troops. Although some were issued to the Home Guard, any unit possessing this weapon could feel highly privileged.

**Browning Automatic Rifle (BAR)** - First was issued to the Home Guard in the summer/autumn of 1940. Of .300 calibre, this weapon also proved popular with members. Twelve BARs were issued to the 4th Battalion as early as August 1940.

**Browning Machine Gun** - Of 1917 vintage, this was issued to the Home Guard at roughly the same time as the Browning Automatic Rifle. Another popular piece of weaponry, Dennis Batten was one member who was "glad these weapons were on our side." Some units mounted these guns on trolleys to make them more mobile.

**EY Rifle** - Specially adapted SMLE rifle. Used for firing grenades, such as Nos 36 or 68 Grenades, from a discharger cup attached to the rifle.(see SMLE and Grenades below). Named after its inventor Edgar Yule. Issued to many units in the early part of 1942. Instructor Sgt A Stenning was killed as a result of an accident at Underhill on March 26th 1944 during training on the use of the EY Rifle. Pte T S Livett MM was seriously wounded. C Company 8th Battalion were under instruction at the time.

**Fougasse** - Built into the roadside this was made from oil or petrol drums containing flammable liquid. An SIP Grenade (see below) was attached, the weapon acting as a fixed position flame thrower or trap when ignited by remote detonator.

**Grenades** - A large selection of Grenades were issued to the Home Guard. Among these were the No.36 anti-personnel Grenade (Mills Bomb), the No.68 (anti-tank) Grenade, No.73 (anti-tank) Grenade, the No.74 Grenade (Sticky Bomb), No. 75 (Hawkins) (anti-tank) Grenade and No. 76 Grenade (The SIP, ie. Self Igniting Phosphorous) Grenade.

**Lee-Metford Rifle** - One of the first weapons to reach the Woking LDV was of Boer War vintage. Issued in very small numbers at first, members taking them on duty often had to hand them in at the end of their patrols so that those going back out had a weapon to carry.

**Lewis Machine Gun** - This was the first machine gun issued to the Home Guard. Ronald Hack remembers one Lewis Gun being issued to each Section of the Farnham LDV. These guns were of WW1 vintage, several being ex-Royal Flying Corps weapons. Those previously used by the RFC had to have a bipod constructed for them before the LDV/Home Guard could use them. Pte Platt of the Hawker Platoon constructed sights and bipods for weapons issued to his unit.

**Molotov Cocktails** - A "home-made" weapon issued to the LDV in the early days. The Molotov was made by filling a bottle that would break on impact (a wine bottle was thought best) with a mixture of petrol, oil and perhaps creosote. The bottle was sealed to prevent the mixture evaporating in storage. Around the neck of the bottle was taped a safety fuse or piece of flammable rag which was lit before the bomb was thrown. On hitting its target the bottle would break and the mixture ignite. These home-made bombs were designed to be used against enemy armoured vehicles and would be aimed at their engine compartments or air intakes, thus striking the vehicle at its most vulnerable point.

**Northover Projector** - The Home Guard's first anti-tank weapon, issued in early 1941. Withdrawn from use in November 1943 the Northover was considered by many to be "rather a Heath Robinson affair". Had a rather strange appearance, having a 'drainpipe' type barrel and being mounted on a tripod. Fired by percussion cap and had a range of about ¼ mile.

**P.14s/P.17s** - The first weapons to be used by the LDV/Home Guard, with the exception of the Molotov Cocktail, these guns arrived from the USA in May 1940 being made by either Springfield, Remington or Eddystone. Part of the Lend-Lease deal set up with the USA. The P.17 was another popular weapon, many regretting its eventual withdrawal.

**Pikes** - Not issued in great numbers to the LDV, despite the legend. Some did find their way to Guildford and Farnham. Soon withdrawn. Despite better weaponry then being available it was the intention to issue pikes to the Home Guard in late 1940 and 1941. This did not happen in many areas, if any.

**Ross Rifle** - A Canadian rifle issued to the LDV in the early days. Prone to jamming and not popular. Despite this problem it was still being used by some units in 1943.

**SMLE (Short Magazine Lee Enfield) Rifles** - Several patterns of this rifle were issued to the LDV/Home Guard, the Mark IIIs being the most popular and quite possibly the best gun issued to the LDV/Home Guard.

**Smith Gun** - First issued to the Home Guard in late 1941/early 1942, the Smith Gun was a highly popular, if somewhat inaccurate, field gun. Many of these were made at the Trianco works in Kingston although a large proportion of later models of this gun were made at Ordnance Factories. Among the units to be issued with this weapon was the Woking based James Walker Factory Platoon who built up a good reputation for the use of the three Smith Guns in their armoury.

**Sten Gun** - Described as a "light handy weapon with a high rate of fire and accuracy at short ranges" the Sten Gun was first issued to the Home Guard in 1942. "Cheap and cheerful" according to Ronald Hack, the Sten Gun was mass produced. Not a particularly attractive looking weapon, the Sten had to be handled very carefully to avoid its falling apart! Carried mainly by Officers and NCOs. Fired a 9mm cartridge.

**Thompson Sub-Machine Gun** - Issued to some units by the early part of 1941, the Thompson was a highly effective machine gun. Its attributes were recognised by the authorities and many of the weapons were later recalled and issued to regular troops. Replaced by the less popular Sten Gun. Ray Lowther of Chertsey remembers "the sensation when a Tommy Gun arrived at the Drill Hall. Previously we had only seen one in the hands of Humphrey Bogart or Edward G Robinson on the silver screen in one of the then popular gangster movies."

**2lb Anti-Tank Gun** - First issued to Home Guards during 1943. This weapon reached Woking a bit too late, units there not receiving the gun until September 1944, about the time that the stand down order was given!

**Vickers Machine Gun** - A popular medium/heavy machine gun, the Vickers was issued to most units in early 1942. The historian of the 4th (Guildford) Battalion, though remembers his Battalion being issued with the weapon in February 1941. Another popular weapon of WW1 vintage. Replaced by the Browning Machine Gun.

*Members of the Walton On The Hill HG Parade in their greatcoats. (Mrs A Haine)*

*A Lewis Gun being demonstrated by a member of the Southern Railway's Home Guard. (Southern Railway/Surrey History Centre)*

*Northover Projectors being used during a Southern Railway exercise in Guildford during 1943. (Surrey History Centre)*

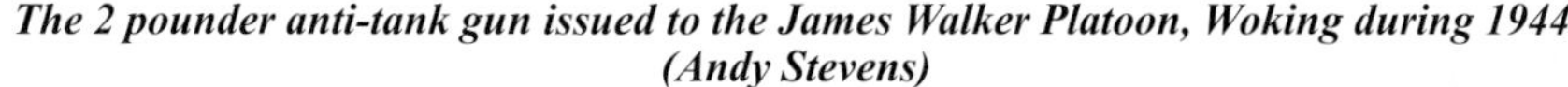

*The 2 pounder anti-tank gun issued to the James Walker Platoon, Woking during 1944. (Andy Stevens)*

# CHAPTER TWELVE -

# THE FINAL DAYS

## STAND DOWN

By the summer of 1944 the end of the Home Guard was in sight. With Allied troops in Northern France and with Germany now on the defensive it began to be recognised that having a home defence force such as the Home Guard was somewhat unnecessary (One of the duties undertaken by the Woking Home Guard was guarding German prisoners of war on their journey from Woking Station to Botley Park Hospital, Chobham where they were to be detained for the duration). Soon came the order that parades were no longer to be made compulsory and that training was to be done on a voluntary basis.

Many members felt that the Home Guard was being allowed to pass into history rather too early and without the recognition that many felt was due to its members. Letters to "The Times" newspaper that month reflect this feeling, with one particular letter from a gentleman signing himself merely as "Company Commander" sparking several more in reply. Not everyone agreed with "Company Commander's" feelings. One member from Esher had obviously had his fill of the Home Guard and wrote to the paper with a somewhat different opinion to that of the earlier correspondent, evidently quite pleased that he could revert to his peacetime lifestyle.

Many members had experienced long hours at work and on duty with the Home Guard but most just got on with it without complaining. One such willing member was Sgt A Howe, ex-C.Q.M.S of the 59th Surrey Battalion. Soon after the Home Guard was stood down Sgt Howe wrote that his work with the unit "represented the third whole time job I was trying to hold down simultaneously, the other two being my job at the Bank and the running of my personal Insurance and Mortgage business. The three jobs together meant an average of some 18 hours per day, but the strain soon passes."

On September 6th 1944 the order was given that the Home Guard was to be stood down on December 31st that year.

A lot of Home Guards were very disappointed with the manner in which the end of the force came. Mrs Isla Franks was also a member of the 59th Surrey (Addington) Battalion and remembers the reaction of members in her unit to that stand down order in the autumn of 1944. "The volunteers were so depressed and disillusioned that they would arrive at HQ and throw their uniforms on the floor in disgust, and I felt rather like that myself. I left before the Home Guard was stood down, it was just too depressing."

The Home Guard's final parade was to be held in London on December 3rd 1944, each Battalion sending a number of representatives to take part in the day's events. Among those to join the parade were Lt Col N H H Ralston, L/Cpl E F Mitchell and Pte G Whittingham (51st Battalion), Capt G J Bullard, Sgt R D Fidler and Pte E A Cooke (52nd Battalion), Major D Freeman, Sgt W S Bird and Pte S J Stockwell (53rd Battalion) and Major T Crowley, Cpl A W Taylor and Pte E J Coward (64th Battalion). Eleven Home Guard bands from across the UK took part in the procession. The parade marched to Hyde Park where the salute was taken by King George VI, the Home Guard's Commander in Chief. The battalions, though, wanted to mark the passing of the Home Guard in their own areas and all arranged to hold local farewell parades during October, November and December 1944.

One of the first Battalions to hold such a parade was the 64th Surrey (Kingston) Battalion. Their parade was held on Sunday October 29th, the salute being taken at the Guildhall by the Mayor of Kingston, Sir Edward Scarles.

The 63rd Surrey (Richmond) Battalion held its final parade on November 5th. It was a very wet day. The Battalion paraded in Richmond Park where it was inspected by the South West London Sub-District Commander, Brigadier F A V Copland-Griffiths DSO MC and the Sector Commander. The Battalion paraded through the park and saluted the memory of fallen comrades from the First World War as they passed the Star and Garter Home for disabled soldiers and sailors. The Battalion then filled Richmond Theatre where it was addressed by several local dignitaries as well as Brigadier Nation, a former Zone Commander. Former Battalion Commanders Colonel and Sir Geoffrey Evans were also present. Saying that he considered all could be proud of their service in the Home Guard, Battalion Commander Colonel Redfearn recalled one occasion when local Civil Defence authorities had searched for a long time to find out the name of a Home Guard member who had given particularly valiant service during one incident, quoting it as an example of the selfless assistance given by many of the members. He also recalled a conversation with a man who had been in the Richmond area for 10 years and had known no one, but having joined the Home Guard in 1943 had now made many friends in the area. Such was the comradeship in the Home Guard. At the end of the ceremony the Battalion marched to the drill hall where they were finally dismissed.

In Farnham members of the Civil Defence services, the British Red Cross Society and the Girls Training Corps formed a guard of honour for members of A Company 2nd Surrey (Farnham) Battalion as they marched to Castle Street behind their Commanding Officer, Major H C Patrick for their last parade on November 26th. The local newspaper later wrote that "(the Battalion), like old soldiers, just 'faded away'. Their spirit will live, however, and the gratitude of the townspeople, exemplified at the stand down parade, will remain evergreen."

Members of the Croydon Home Guard marched past the Lord Lieutenant during their parade on November 26th, the individual Battalions holding their own parades a week later.

Most parades were held on Sunday 3rd December. Writing after the war in 'Soldiers of the King', a history of the 53rd Battalion, Lt Col R A Pepperall made special mention of the many veterans of the early days of the LDV who attended the Battalion's farewell parade. Members of outlying Platoons were transported to Cranleigh for the farewell parade of the 5th Surrey (Bramley) Battalion, where 1000 Officers, NCOs and men were joined by 49 of the Battalion's women auxiliaries. The close liaison between the Home Guard and the local Civil Defence services was acknowledged by the Battalion Commander, Lt Col E R Hopewell, before he took the final salute on the village cricket ground. Whether or not to wear gas capes as protection against the rain seems to have been a major concern in Reigate and Redhill as the parade of the 8th Surrey (Reigate) Battalion became one of the many to suffer from the inclement weather across the country that weekend.

Colonel Redfearn's comments on the spirit of fellowship built up within the Home Guard were repeated by Colonel G W Geddes during the final parade of the 4th Surrey (Guildford) Battalion during their final parade on December 3rd 1944. He also had a message for the future. Addressing the members of his Battalion at the Technical College Ground, Col Geddes said that they all should "carry the standard of this comradeship on to the days of peace, when it comes, and try to make the life of the future on the same level as we did in our Battalion days".

Over 1000 attended the parade in Guildford and heard Col Geddes say that the parade should not only be seen as the Battalion's Stand Down parade but also as a Remembrance parade, to commemorate all the Battalion had achieved over the last 4 ½ years. He also reminded the men that they were only being stood down, not disbanded and as such were liable to be recalled at any time. Col Geddes told the battalion that it had been an honour and privilege to have led those under his command in the Home Guard and received three cheers at the end of the parade before taking the final salute.

Bands accompanied many of the farewell parades. In Richmond the parade of the 63rd Battalion had been led by the band of the East Surrey Regiment whilst the band of the Queen's Royal Regiment accompanied the 4th Battlaion at their parade in Guildford. In Woking two bands provided the music for the 11th Battalion's parade on Wheatsheaf Common, where the Royal Canadian Band were joined by members of the Woking Army Cadet Force Band. Attended by over 700 Home Guards, the parade was inspected by the Battalion Commander, Sir Alan Bourne.

Many Platoons and Companies held their own functions to mark the stand down. G Company (Oxshott) 6th Surrey (Leatherhead) Battalion held a smoking concert in their Drill Hall on Saturday October 28th. Those attending heard the Commanding Officer, Major Warwick Gregory, praise the support of member's wives, saying that they "had for so long and so often been deprived of the company of their menfolk." In Hindhead, a similar function was held by members of No.3 Platoon E Company 2nd Surrey (Farnham) Battalion at the local British Legion Club on Saturday 9th December. At the farewell dinner of No.9 Platoon A Company 51st Surrey (Malden) Battalion the

Battalion's Commanding Officer, Lt Col N H H Ralston described the Home Guard as "one of the seven wonders of the world."

## IN RECOGNITION

Awards such as those given to members of the 12th Battalion were not the only ones members were eligible to receive when the Home Guard was stood down. Although many regretted that a special Home Guard medal was never to be distributed, those who had served for three years or more in home defence bodies qualified for the Defence Medal, 1939-1945. Members also received a certificate to commemorate their time in the force. The King's Birthday and New Honours Lists had always provided commanders with the opportunity to award those who had served with distinction in the Home Guard , as has been seen in a previous chapter. Many now received recognition for their work with the force by the award of the OBE or British Empire Medal. Amongst those so honoured at this time were Lt Col G E W Lane (7th Battalion) (OBE), Lt Col N H H Ralston (51st Battalion) (OBE) and Lt Col G H Ward (60th Battalion) (OBE). Others to receive the OBE included Captain W D Kennedy of the 221st Rocket Anti-Aircraft Battery and Major J W B Farmer (11th Battalion), whilst the BEM was awarded to, amongst others, Sgt M M Devaney (1st Battalion), Sgt H E Freeman (3rd Battalion), Pte T Briscoe (55th Battalion) and Pte H S Hayward (71st Surrey Heavy Anti-Aircraft Battery). This was also the final chance for members to receive Certificates for Good Conduct (or Gallantry) from their Commanding Officer.

Meanwhile, in Weybridge, one Officer had already decided that a Home Guard medal should have been awarded. At a smoking concert held at Oatlands Park Hotel on November 3rd he displayed his effort, as part of a fund raising event for the Red Cross. The Surrey Comet reported that the medal had "a long ribbon consisting of red tape together with a number of bars (or clasps) representing the places where the Company had been in action, such as the Jolly Farmer, the Hand and Spear and other well known hostelries."

## PRESS CALL

The press were always quite supportive of the LDV/Home Guard. In the early days, many column inches were given over to news of how the new force was progressing. Details of the numbers enrolled were often given week by week and whenever the LDV needed something, such as the loan of private arms or clothing for the winter, the local press helped out by printing appeals within its pages. Later on, the annual anniversaries of the forming of the LDV were faithfully reported, especially the 3rd anniversary, coverage of which must have run into several hundred pages up and down the country.

There were obviously restrictions on just how much detail the papers could include. Reports on incidents during the Battle of Britain, for instance, usually failed to include a place name in case sensitive information reached the wrong hands. However, whenever possible, the press continued to give the public as much information as it could about the country's part-time army. The Surrey Mirror carried the report on the Reigate Fieldcraft School during 1943, whilst the Guildford based Surrey Advertiser told its readers all about the local Battalion's exercise in the town during May 1942. Court cases were also reported, as were events such as dances, weddings and funerals. Plenty of space was also given to reports on the Home Guard's stand down parades in December 1944.

Publications such as 'Sunday Pictorial', 'War Illustrated' and 'Picture Post' also gave good coverage to the Home Guard. News from around the Battalion was also given in 'Defence-The Services Magazine and Home Guard Monthly'. Individual units had also issued magazines or newspapers to their members to keep them up to date with Home Guard news. Members of the various railway Battalions were particularly fortunate in that all of the 'big four' published in house magazines during the war. The Southern Railway also issued a free newspaper specifically covering its Home Guards activities. Shortly after the Home Guard was stood down the company published a booklet entitled 'Home Guard Southern Railway In Pictures', a quite excellent publication containing numerous pictures of the railway's Home Guard in action.

Many other Home Guard Battalions now set about recording their unit's story, both for the benefit of the general public and for their own members. Several had kept diaries of their activities, although many of these do not seem to have survived the ravages of time. In October 1944, the 'Sutton and Cheam Herald' published a two part history of the 55th Surrey (Sutton and Cheam) Battalion. This was later published as a single edition booklet and made available to the general public, suggested minimum price 6d. The profits from the sale of the booklet would go towards the 'Mayor's fund for the endowment of a cot in the Children's Ward of the Sutton and Cheam Hospital in the name of the 55th Battalion'. (The 63rd Battalion would also endow a bed to their local hospital). The 'Surrey Mirror' would follow suit in January 1945 by publishing the story of its own local Battalion, the 8th Surrey (Reigate) Battalion. This piece was essentially an abridged version of a full length book published at round about the same time. Several other Surrey Battalions arranged for the publication of books detailing their history. Among these were the 4th (Guildford), 51st (Malden), 53rd (Weston Green) (entitled 'Soldiers of the King'), 58th (Purley) and 63rd (Richmond) Battalions. The story of E Company, 5th Surrey (Cranleigh) Battalion, was also recorded.

## AT PEACE

To some the end of the Home Guard meant an end to an exciting period of their lives, one when they had been given perhaps a final chance to do something for their country and for themselves. When the end came many found new outlets into which to channel their energies. Sgt F C Reid was awarded a Certificate for Good Conduct for his work with the 59th Surrey Battalion and wrote to his former Commanding Officer, Lt Col H G Pierce to thank him for the award. Expressing the view of his former colleagues under Lt Col Pierce, Sgt Reid wrote "I, with many others, will always look back on our service under you as a great stepping stone in our lives, and to me it was a most interesting and in many ways enjoyable period of my life, for which we owe thanks to you and your Officers. I have been shaken out of the lethargy of civilian life and am now trying to continue interesting activity in the Cadet Force."

For others the stand down of the Home Guard was a sadder time.

Isla Franks recalls a chance meeting with a former Home Guard colleague sometime after the war. "About a year later, while walking in Croydon, I saw a figure coming towards me dressed in an old raincoat, a cap on his head and carrying a canvas shopping bag which seemed too heavy for him. Just an ordinary old man. There was just something slightly familiar about him which made me look twice. His face lit up in recognition. "How are you my dear? It's nice to see you again." I searched his face. "Why Corporal it's you, how are you keeping?" We chatted about old times, old friends – it already seemed so long ago. After a while he said "must be getting back to my dinner. I just can't stand these cold winds. It's my arthritis, you know, had it for years, but mustn't grumble, I'll be 60 next month." I remembered the last time I had seen him, just over a year previously, manhandling boxes of ammunition into the back of a truck, shouting at men 10 years younger than himself to "get a move on, we haven't got all day, put your backs into it!" His uniform was gleaming, shoulders and arms moving with ease. "Take care Corporal" I said "Lovely to see you again." But it wasn't".

## THE HOME GUARD SPIRIT

The Home Guard had always been a pretty highly disciplined body of men and women. There were a few exceptions, though. Cases of absenteeism from parade were sometimes brought before the civil courts, as were occasional cases involving the of misuse of Home Guard petrol. Some members were even dismissed as being unsuitable for the Home Guard, but such instances were fortunately fairly rare.

There has been some doubt cast recently over the number of Home Guard casualties during the war. The figures generally accepted to be more or less correct, however, are that some 1206 were to die as a result of injuries sustained on duty whilst 557 were injured. There are lasting memorials to those who died. The Commonwealth War Graves Commission, initially set up in 1917 to look after the graves of those who died during the First World War, maintains the graves of a few Home Guards killed during the second great conflict. Amongst those graves it looks after are those of 11 members of the 57th Battalion killed as a result of an air-raid on Mitcham in April 1941, the grave of Sgt. Arthur Stenning of the 8th Battalion (died 26th March 1944) and that of Private Eric Bathurst, 2nd Surrey (Farnham) Battalion, who died on 10th October 1943. The grave of Platoon Commander

W Battle, who, as mentioned in a previous chapter, died on August 18th 1940 is also maintained by the commission. Many Home Guards left to join the regular forces, and graves of those former members who died on active service are also tended by the Commission. These include that of Albert Tilyard-Burrows, who died in the fighting around Normandy on 27th July 1944. Tilyard-Burrows had previously been a recipient of the George Medal whilst a member of the Vickers Aircraft Home Guard, 3rd Surrey (Weybridge) Battalion, for his actions during an attack on the factory at Brooklands on September 21st 1941.

December 1944 did not see the end of the Home Guard spirit as the comradeship spoken about by Lt Cols Redfearn and Geddes now rose to the fore. No. 15 Platoon D Company 8th Surrey (Reigate) Platoon organised a reunion of its members as early as March 1945, members taking the opportunity to present their Platoon Commander Lt W B Parker with a leather brief case after dinner at the Warwick Hotel, Redhill. Several Battalions or Platoons formed Home Guard clubs; many of them survive to this day as rifle clubs. One such club, the 32nd and 61st Surrey Home Guard Rifle and Pistol Club was formed in Croydon, although not too many of its current day members are ex-Home Guards. A Battalion Club was also formed by members of the 63rd Surrey (Richmond) Battalion, members meeting every Wednesday and Sunday. Amongst the facilities offered to members were billiards, darts and table tennis whilst some members formed a Golf Society and competed for an in-house trophy. A similar association was formed by members of the 39th County of London (Metropolitan Water Board) Battalion in Walton-on-Thames, the rules of the club stating that its object was to "cement a comradeship formed during the period of service in No.11 Platoon, Walton." The annual subscription to the club was 2s 6d (now 12 ½p).

Several towns and villages had British Legion Clubs (a lot still do) and many ex-Home Guards now wanted to join. However, as membership of the clubs was normally restricted to those of a military background, many debates were held as to whether Home Guards should be allowed to join. One such debate was held at the AGM of the Puttenham and Wanborough British Legion in November 1944. This meeting had a successful outcome for the towns' Home Guards as a resolution that they should be accepted into the club was passed by those present.

Some of the more specialist sections of the Home Guard sought to put their skills to good use in peacetime. In January 1945 ex-motor cycle dispatch riders from the 54th Surrey (Wimbledon) Battalion formed the Wimbledon and District Motor Cycle Club at the Drill Hall, St Georges Road and in September 1945 started training learners in a rented field at Mitcham. The Club eventually became the pioneers of the RAC/ACU National Training Scheme.

## REFORMED AND RE-ARMED

The Home Guard was disbanded on 31st December 1945. That was still not the end of the force, however as in 1952 it was reformed to help guard against a possible threat from Russia. This time round there was a distinct lack of enthusiasm for the force, the majority of those volunteering being members of Home Guard Rifle Clubs as barely 30,000 'joined up' across the UK. The Home Guard lasted in this diluted form until July 1957 when it was disbanded for probably the last time.

The summer of 1998 saw the Home Guard make one final attempt to grab the headlines in Surrey. Builders working on the site of the former Crosby Doors factory in Crosby Way, Farnham uncovered a 2000lb bomb causing West Street in the town centre to be evacuated at 3pm on Wednesday July 22nd. Six bomb disposal experts were called out to investigate before it was decided that the bomb was a training device used by Home Guards, probably in Farnham Park. It contained no explosives but it was 8 hours before those evacuated from their homes were allowed to return.

## IN MEMORIAM

There are at least two permanent reminders of the Home Guard in Surrey. In the church of St Mary the Blessed Virgin, Addington Village, Croydon is a stained glass window dedicated to the memory of the local Battalion. The inscription on the window reads 'To the Glory of God and as a memorial of their service to King and Country by members of the 59th Surrey (Addington) Battalion Home Guard this window is erected 1952'.

Finally, on June 6th 1999 a special service was held at Guildford Cathedral during which two windows were dedicated to the county's Home Guard. The windows commemorate the battalions affiliated to the Queen's Royal Regiment and the East Surrey Regiment, the service being arranged by the Queen's Royal Regimental Association. The service was attended by many former members of the Surrey Battalions. The dedication, read by the Dean of Guildford Cathedral was as follows:

*"Almighty God, the God of righteousness and peace: We render thanks to thee for the courage and devotion of those prepared to defend our country in its hour of need, especially the members of the Home Guard serving in this county of Surrey; may these windows, which we dedicate in thy Name, be a reminder to us of their service, that succeeding generations may honour their vigilance and uphold the freedoms they pledged to defend."*

A fitting and lasting tribute to the men and women of the Surrey Home Guard.

STAND-DOWN PARTY
Royal Albert Hall
At 6.30 p.m.
For members of the Home Guard only

Given by the following artists:—
TOMMY TRINDER
CICELY COURTNEIDGE
VERA LYNN
GEORGE ROBEY and VIOLET LORAINE
BENNETT & WILLIAMS
JOSE FEARON and CHARLES GILLESPIE
ELSIE & DORIS WATERS
ROB WILTON
AND
LOUIS LEVY with his Band of Fifty and a Chorus of Thirty with MONIA LITER.

HOME GUARD
Farewell
PARADE
HYDE PARK
At 3 p.m.
AND
STAND-DOWN PARTY
ROYAL ALBERT HALL
At 6.30 p.m.

SUNDAY, 3rd DECEMBER 1944.

SOUVENIR
PROGRAMME

***Programme for the Stand Down events at Hyde Park and The Royal Albert Hall, December 3rd 1944. (Jim Ponsford)***

***Croydon Home Guards march past large crowds during their final parade on December 3rd 1944. (Reproduced by kind permission of the Croydon Advertiser Group)***

The Under-Secretary of State for War presents his compliments and by Command of the Army Council has the honour to transmit the enclosed Awards granted for service during the war of 1939-45.

*The Defence Medal awarded to George Crook. (Paul Crook)*

*George Crook's Home Guard certificate. (Alan Crook)*

*(top right)*
*Guildford Cathedral stained glass windows, dedicated on June 6th 1999. (Surrey Advertiser)*

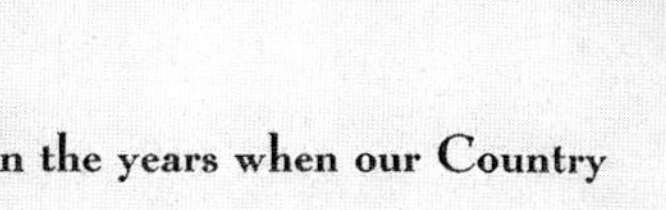

In the years when our Country was in mortal danger

George CROOK

who served 17 July 1940 - 20 October 1942
17 December 1943 - 31 December 1944

gave generously of his time and powers to make himself ready for her defence by force of arms and with his life if need be.

George R.I.

THE HOME GUARD

***The author's father, Alan Crook, at the Mitcham graves of 11 Home Guards killed on the night of April 16th/17th 1941. (Paul Crook)***

***The grave of HF Langbein, 57th Battalion, Mitcham. (Paul Crook)***

# SELECTED BIBLIOGRAPHY

**Books etc:**

Dad's Army in Caterham - Jean Tooke
Guildford at War – Surrey Advertiser
Sussex Home Guard – Paul Crook
War on the Line – Bernard Darwin
Croydon and the Second World War
Giles at War – Peter Tory
The Real Dad's Army – Norman Longmate
The Home Guard of Britain – Charles Graves
Hazardous Work – J D Sainsbury
Soldiers of the King – The History of the 53rd Surrey Battalion
Surrey at War – Bob Ogley
Ewhurst – The Ewhurst Historical Society
Stand To Woking – Andy Stevens
Britons To Arms – G A Steppler
The Home Guard – S P Mackenzie
The Home Guard – David Carroll
Dorking At War – D Knight
Are We At War (Letters to The Times 1939 to 1945)
Surrey Airfields in the Second World War – Len Pilkington
Our Home Front – Surrey Heath Museum
Raiders Overhead – Stephen Fowler
The Battle of Britain – Richard Hough and Denis Richards
London Transport at War 1939 to 1945 – Charles Graves
First World War – Martin Gilbert
The Penguin Book of The Second World War – P Calvocoressi, G Wint & J Pritchard
Ellermans, A Wealth of Shipping – James Taylor
Stand Down – L B Whittaker
It All Happened Before – Radnor & Cooper
Wings Over Brooklands – Howard Johnson
British Army Uniforms and Insignia – Brian Davis
A Summer For Heroes – Derek Wood with Derek Dempster
Under The Guns of The Red Baron – N Franks, H Giblin & N McCrery
The Battle of Britain Then and Now (Vols 1 & 2) – After The Battle

**Newspapers:**

Surrey Advertiser
Surrey Mirror
Croydon Times
Croydon Advertiser
Farnham Herald
Aldershot and Farnborough News and Mail
Woking News and Mail
Surrey Comet

# INDEX TO PLACES

**Easebourne Lane, Midhurst, W Sussex.** GU29 9AZ **Tel: 01730 813169 Fax: 01730 812601**
***If books are not available from your local transport stockist, order direct with cheque, Visa or Mastercard, post free UK.***

## BRANCH LINES
Branch Line to Allhallows
Branch Line to Alton
Branch Lines around Ascot
Branch Line to Ashburton
Branch Lines around Bodmin
Branch Line to Bude
Branch Lines around Canterbury
Branch Lines around Chard & Yeovil
Branch Lines around Cromer
Branch Lines to East Grinstead
Branch Lines of East London
Branch Lines to Effingham Junction
Branch Lines around Exmouth
Branch Line to Fairford
Branch Lines around Gosport
Branch Line to Hawkhurst
Branch Lines to Horsham
Branch Lines around Huntingdon
Branch Line to Ilfracombe
Branch Line to Kingswear
Branch Lines to Launceston & Princetown
Branch Lines to Longmoor
Branch Line to Looe
Branch Line to Lyme Regis
Branch Lines around March
Branch Lines around Midhurst
Branch Line to Minehead
Branch Line to Moretonhampstead
Branch Line to Padstow
Branch Lines around Plymouth
Branch Lines to Seaton and Sidmouth
Branch Line to Selsey
Branch Lines around Sheerness
Branch Line to Shrewsbury
Branch Line to Swanage *updated*
Branch Line to Tenterden
Branch Lines to Torrington
Branch Lines to Tunbridge Wells
Branch Line to Upwell
Branch Lines of West London
Branch Lines around Weymouth
Branch Lines around Wisbech

## NARROW GAUGE BRANCH LINES
Branch Line to Lynton
Branch Lines around Portmadoc 1923-46
Branch Lines around Porthmadog 1954-94
Branch Line to Southwold
Douglas to Port Erin
Kent Narrow Gauge
Two-Foot Gauge Survivors
Romneyrail
Southern France Narrow Gauge
Vivarais Narrow Gauge

## SOUTH COAST RAILWAYS
Ashford to Dover
Bournemouth to Weymouth
Brighton to Eastbourne
Brighton to Worthing
Dover to Ramsgate
Eastbourne to Hastings
Hastings to Ashford
Portsmouth to Southampton
Southampton to Bournemouth

## SOUTHERN MAIN LINES
Basingstoke to Salisbury
Bromley South to Rochester
Crawley to Littlehampton
Dartford to Sittingbourne
East Croydon to Three Bridges
Epsom to Horsham
Exeter to Barnstaple
Exeter to Tavistock
Faversham to Dover
London Bridge to East Croydon
Orpington to Tonbridge
Tonbridge to Hastings
Salisbury to Yeovil
Swanley to Ashford
Tavistock to Plymouth
Victoria to East Croydon
Waterloo to Windsor
Waterloo to Woking
Woking to Portsmouth
Woking to Southampton
Yeovil to Exeter

## EASTERN MAIN LINES
Fenchurch Street to Barking
Ipswich to Saxmundham
Liverpool Street to Ilford

## WESTERN MAIN LINES
Ealing to Slough
Ely to Kings Lynn
Exeter to Newton Abbot
Paddington to Ealing
Slough to Newbury

## COUNTRY RAILWAY ROUTES
Andover to Southampton
Bath Green Park to Bristol
Bath to Evercreech Junction
Bournemouth to Evercreech Jn.
Cheltenham to Andover
Croydon to East Grinstead
Didcot to Winchester
East Kent Light Railway
Fareham to Salisbury
Frome to Bristol
Guildford to Redhill
Reading to Basingstoke
Reading to Guildford
Redhill to Ashford
Salisbury to Westbury
Stratford upon Avon to Cheltenham
Strood to Paddock Wood
Taunton to Barnstaple
Wenford Bridge to Fowey
Westbury to Bath
Woking to Alton
Yeovil to Dorchester

## GREAT RAILWAY ERAS
Ashford from Steam to Eurostar
Clapham Junction 50 years of change
Festiniog in the Fifties
Festiniog in the Sixties
Isle of Wight Lines 50 years of change
Railways to Victory 1944-46
SECR Centenary album
Talyllyn 50 years of change
Yeovil 50 years of change

## LONDON SUBURBAN RAILWAYS
Caterham and Tattenham Corner
Charing Cross to Dartford
Clapham Jn. to Beckenham Jn.
Crystal Palace (HL) & Catford Loop
East London Line
Finsbury Park to Alexandra Palace
Kingston and Hounslow Loops
Lewisham to Dartford
Lines around Wimbledon
London Bridge to Addiscombe
Mitcham Junction Lines
North London Line
South London Line
West Croydon to Epsom
West London Line
Willesden Junction to Richmond
Wimbledon to Epsom

## STEAMING THROUGH
Steaming through Cornwall
Steaming through the Isle of Wight
Steaming through Kent
Steaming through West Hants
Steaming through West Sussex

## TRAMWAY CLASSICS
Aldgate & Stepney Tramways
Barnet & Finchley Tramways
Bath Tramways
Bournemouth & Poole Tramways
Brighton's Tramways
Burton & Ashby Tramways
Camberwell & W.Norwood Tramways
Clapham & Streatham Tramways
Croydon's Tramways
Dover's Tramways
East Ham & West Ham Tramways
Edgware and Willesden Tramways
Eltham & Woolwich Tramways
Embankment & Waterloo Tramways
Enfield & Wood Green Tramways
Exeter & Taunton Tramways
Greenwich & Dartford Tramways
Hammersmith & Hounslow Tramways
Hampstead & Highgate Tramways
Hastings Tramways
Holborn & Finsbury Tramways
Ilford & Barking Tramways
Kingston & Wimbledon Tramways
Lewisham & Catford Tramways
Liverpool Tramways 1. Eastern Routes
Liverpool Tramways 2. Southern Routes
Liverpool Tramways 3. Northern Routes
Maidstone & Chatham Tramways
Margate to Ramsgate
North Kent Tramways
Norwich Tramways
Portsmouth's Tramways
Reading Tramways
Seaton & Eastbourne Tramways
Shepherds Bush & Uxbridge Tramways
Southampton Tramways
Southend-on-sea Tramways
Southwark & Deptford Tramways
Stamford Hill Tramways
Twickenham & Kingston Tramways
Victoria & Lambeth Tramways
Waltham Cross & Edmonton Tramways
Walthamstow & Leyton Tramways
Wandsworth & Battersea Tramways

## TROLLEYBUS CLASSICS
Croydon Trolleybuses
Bournemouth Trolleybuses
Hastings Trolleybuses
Maidstone Trolleybuses
Reading Trolleybuses
Woolwich & Dartford Trolleybuses

## WATERWAY ALBUMS
Kent and East Sussex Waterways
London to Portsmouth Waterway
West Sussex Waterways

## MILITARY BOOKS
Battle over Portsmouth
Battle over Sussex 1940
Blitz over Sussex 1941-42
Bombers over Sussex 1943-45
Bognor at War
Military Defence of West Sussex
Military Signals from the South Coast
Secret Sussex Resistance
Surrey Home Guard
Sussex Home Guard

## OTHER RAILWAY BOOKS
Garraway Father & Son
Index to all Middleton Press stations
Industrial Railways of the South-East
South Eastern & Chatham Railways
London Chatham & Dover Railway
War on the Line (SR 1939-45)